LEADEROLOGY

Oleg Konovalov

WildBluePress.com

LEADEROLOGY published by:
WILDBLUE PRESS
P.O. Box 102440
Denver, Colorado 80250

WILDBLUE PRESS is registered at the U.S. Patent and Trademark Offices.

ISBN 978-1-948239-40-0   Trade Paperback
ISBN 978-1-948239-39-4   eBook

Interior Formatting by Elijah Toten
www.totencreative.com

LEADEROLOGY

Praises

"In Leaderology, Oleg Konovalov explores new dimensions of businesses, as well as organizations, culture, and leadership. This book shares the best lessons in modern management!"

—*Marshall Goldsmith, Only two-time Thinkers 50 #1 Leadership Thinker in the world*

"Every once in a while you encounter a book that makes you rethink how you think about management. This is one of those rare gems."

—*Jonas Ridderstråle, Thinkers50, author of Funky Business and Fast/Forward*

"Leaderology explores the wholly workplace trinity of leadership, culture and the organization. The author takes an unconventional and personal approach to these business issues, making them very readable and innovative. I would recommend this book if you are interested in organizational behavior and its consequences for business performance."

—*Professor Sir Cary Cooper, ALLIANCE Manchester Business School, University of Manchester*

"Oleg Konovalov offers an insightful look at the 'holy trinity' that dictates successful management outcomes — company, culture and leadership — and how they unpin customer satisfaction. A useful read for executives across sectors and geographies."

—*Courtney Fingar, Editor-in-Chief, fDi Magazine, FT Specialist*

"I have learned that purpose driven, passionate people guided by values that empower and protect them create amazing outcomes. In this book, Oleg Konovalov doesn't just highlight what competencies are needed operationally; he points out the value of culture and what good leadership practices look like. Today purpose and values both unlock the passion of people and protect them by building trust. You will be better equipped to build an enduring company that creates value for its people, its customers, and its shareholders after reading Dr. Konovalov's work. This is an incredibly valuable and timely book for all leaders aiming to build enduring businesses."

—*Garry Ridge, CEO – WD-40 Company*

"Leaderology is a compendium that every CEO, Leader, Entrepreneur, and Professor should read. It provides an overarching view of what an organization should be and provides the drivers to make it succeed. Dr. Konovalov then provides the details to ensure that execution occurs to produce the desired results. Leaderology is a magnificent body of work. To put it mildly, it is a Masterpiece!"

—*Dr. Terry Jackson, CEO of JCG Consulting Group LLC, Marshall Goldsmith 100 Coach.*

"In his new book, Oleg Konovalov gives business leaders a wake-up call for the new digital reality. He'll show you how to avoid pitfalls in building successful businesses and radically improve your performance."

—*Dorie Clark, author of Reinventing You and Stand Out, adjunct professor at Duke University Fuqua School of Business*

"A practical, painstaking and personal journey through the multiple facets of business."

—*Emmanuel Gobillot, Author of Unleash Your Leader*

"Oleg Konovalov continues to push new thinking about leaders and business. His expert passion for people, innovation and leadership - critical ingredients for excellence - is contagious."

—*Terence Mauri, Thinkers50 Radar, Inc. Magazine columnist, author of The Leader's Mindset*

"Oleg Konovalov's Leaderology offers tested strategies for handling everything from organizational misalignment to exploring problems with vision, culture, and engagement. With practical tips and case studies, Oleg paints a vivid picture of what we must learn about what we don't know about our organizations. This book is for any leader who wants to create significant value, avoid mistakes, and prepare a dynamic culture for their organization. The best lessons for ultimate business success."

—*Dr. Diane Hamilton, Founder and CEO of Tonerra*

"With the increasing need to adapt to new realities faster while engineering innovative solutions to customers in a way that promotes positive impact on people and planet, the role of business has changed and Dr. Oleg Konovalov's 'Leaderology' offers a timely reflection on organization, culture and leadership. The world needs authentic leadership that connects and serves people attuned to a higher purpose. Inspiring reminder that we are responsible for the future we create."

—*Adriana Machado, Founder at Briyah Institute, Former CEO at GE Brazil*

"Dr. Konovalov's new book on the three core elements of business (organization, its culture, and leadership), as well as the fourth element (customer demand), should be required reading for every business owner—those just starting out as well as those who are well seasoned. Invaluable lessons for reaching new height in business performance."

—Barbara Weltman, Founder/President at Big Ideas for Small Business® Inc.

"I see Oleg Konovalov's new book as an immense compass for leaders, foreseeing the elements of culture and leadership phenomenon. The book itself describes the importance and necessity of the leader-context relationship including customer and future point of views. Leaderology is a source book of successful leaders."

—Didem Gürcüoğlu Tekay, Senior Partner at Management Centre Turkey

"Dr. Oleg Konovalov gives great insights on building an amazing company. The three pillars of organization, culture, and leadership are spot on for doing business in the 21st century! A great read for anyone who wants to genuinely see the success of their business going into the future!"

—Karin Volo, Chief Joy Bringer / CEO of Evoloshen Academy, bestselling author of Engage!

"Dr. Oleg Konovalov has stitched together some of the best leadership ideas and tips I have seen in more than 35 years in business! I would liken him to a younger version of one of my all-time favorite management thinkers, namely, the mighty Peter F Drucker! I am highly impressed by Leaderology's generosity, grace and wisdom all based on common sense observations. This book is an absolute MUST read for any leader interested in becoming or simply being a leader who is future-ready."

—*Andrew Nowak, Leadership, Executive & Team Coach, Marshall Goldsmith 100 Coach*

"This book should be called the 'Konovalov Kaleidoscope of Competence'. It captivatingly condenses the lessons every manager attains only after a lifetime of experience, and yet which every aspiring and developing manager would benefit from knowing in advance. His 'Thirty Lessons on Leadership' alone, exquisitely encapsulates a medley of leadership acumen that all managers would be best served to understand; from the factory floor to those beyond the boardroom door."

—*Noel Ferguson, Executive Chairman, Institute of One World Leadership*

"Leadership is easy. We each make it hard by forgetting our humanity and that of invited collaborators in achieving values-driven vision(s). The principles have been known for centuries, nay millennia across cultures in which many elements changed.

There are three things any organization (public, private or NFP/NGO) needs to get right. The vision spectrum through to its customer(s). The customer chain of trust back through the organization. The continuous improvement pathways across the vision and chain of trust. Do this right through developing people and the culture will flourish; as will the organization.

Dr. Oleg Konovalov sets people on this journey to deal well with the elements for organizational success, including essential lifetime learning for each person. By stepping through elements that make any organization agile and successful in mission we are reminded of those long-known principles. I recommend a reflective read and embedment into daily life for everyone, not just for people in or aspiring to positional leadership/management positions."

—*Neville Garnham, CEO and MD Today4tomorrow Group Pty Ltd., Australia*

Table of Contents

Foreword

It is a profound honor to have been asked to write the foreword to this book. During my thirty-year career as a CEO, consultant, and executive coach I have read more than 2,500 business books. In recent years, after being recognized as one of the top business experts in the world, dozens of authors have asked me to review their work. In 2018, Oleg asked me if I would read his book *Corporate Superpower: Cultivating A Winning Culture For Your Business* and possibly write a quote for the book jacket. I really loved that book and was more than happy to give it a strong recommendation -

"This book is among the most comprehensive, insightful and educational books I've ever read on how to build a world-class culture. I consider this a must read on this extremely critical topic."

Then in early 2019 I got a note from Oleg asking if I would read a draft of this book and consider writing the foreword. I told him that I would only do it if I felt the book was truly excellent. However, this book is not excellent – it is the best business book I have ever read. This is a very serious statement for me, but I have no hesitation in saying it and let me tell you why.

I have a rule that if I get fifty pages into a book and have not highlighted anything, I stop reading it. As I read through the draft of Leaderology I highlighted just the ideas that I found particularly meaningful, yet found myself highlighting almost entire chapters. When I combined my notes of only the sections I had highlighted it totaled thirty-three pages! There were so many times I came across a short phrase that hit me like a thunderbolt, a powerful idea delivered with elegance and simplicity.

I'm a huge fan of Peter Drucker, the father of modern management, and I feel passionately that the ideas in this book are on the same level as Drucker's timeless insights and will have a profound impact on business thinking for years to come.

In this book you will explore Oleg's view that there are four essential elements to any business. Organization, culture, and leadership make up the business itself, and they exist to serve the fourth element – customer demand. He employs the analogy of comparing a business as a living organism and uses the human body as the example for this framework.

"Any organization is alive, much like a human or any other creature. Any company is formed by people to serve people. Organizations should be seen as living entities that can be taught to breathe, function, move and develop inside their specific environments."

Oleg has even developed a new school of thought called "Leaderology," which he defines as

"A leader's serendipity in finding successful strategies, effective solutions and approaches depend on a well-homogenized mixture of vision, competencies, intuition, love, knowledge, focus and concern about others. Here we should think of leaderology, a new but necessary term."

Another key concept in the book is that it is impossible to lead a company successfully if you do not understand the nature of the organization, it's DNA. According to Oleg's typology of business there are five archetypes of organizations – producers, knowledge-dependent, location-dependent, donor-dependent, and state-affiliated organizations. Each of these archetypes demands a different kind of strategy, leadership, culture, and customer relationship. Although this might seem obvious, I have seen many organizations fail because they did not understand what kind of business they were actually trying to run.

Oleg has been recognized as one of the top thought leaders in the world on culture and in this book his sophisticated ideas reflect why he is held in such high regard. I was especially touched by Oleg's philosophies on culture which are rooted in ideas such as humility, caring, respect, responsibility, fellowship, commitment, and love. These are not terms you hear often enough in the business world, but I can assure you that to run a successful organization these must be at the center of everything you do. Some people think that culture is a "touchy – feely" subject, but it has been my experience that in most organizations culture is the area where you can create the greatest improvement in profitability (ROC = Return On Culture) or the fastest route to failure. According to Oleg:

"Culture connects people's hearts and minds in their actions. It serves as a catalyzer of performance making human relations meaningful, productive, and rich in positive emotions whether among colleagues or in relations with customers. It breathes life into formal processes, hierarchical dependencies, and daily routines. Positive culture serves as a ministry of happiness for employees and customers as well."

I have served as an executive coach to companies around the globe from startups to the Fortune 50, and one of my greatest challenges is trying to help a leadership team understand the importance developing a clear, vivid, and compelling vision for the future of the company and the people who work in it. Thanks to Oleg I now have a meaningful way to communicate that concept through this excerpt from his book.

"Vision is a divine gift entrusted to those who will use it to empower others. Vision is a concentration of desires, dreams, potentials, and possibilities. A vision pushes people not just to do more but to do more than they think they are capable of."

This book is Oleg's vision for what it takes to build and sustain a highly successful enterprise.

I implore you to take your time and think deeply about what you are learning. From his life on fishing boats to now lecturing at university, Oleg has gained a unique perspective about how things work in the real world. To use his own analogy, he understands business at a cellular level, and you would do well to take his sage advice.

I am certain that Leaderology will be regarded as one of the most important business books of our time, and I feel fortunate to have the opportunity to play a small part in bringing Dr. Oleg Konovalov's great wisdom to the world.

I wish you every possible happiness and success.

—John Spence, One of the Top 100
business thought leaders in the world

INTRODUCTION

A LETTER TO MYSELF
WHEN I WAS THIRTY

Hi me!

If you are reading this letter, then you are about to celebrate your thirtieth birthday. My congratulations!

Your life is already full of good and bad experiences, inspiring moments, and plenty of encouragement. I am proud seeing how you progressed despite tough obstacles and needing to start over again after many mistakes and failures. However, I don't think you need my praise. What you need, or rather want to know is what mistakes to avoid and what will remain important for many years ahead.

A few years back I found myself in a tough professional crisis after some heavy losses. I was exhausted, losing self-confidence, and had no clear idea where to go. My previous achievements actually held me back, restricting critical thinking and keeping me in a cycle, making the same mental mistakes again and again.

One day I sat with a cup of coffee and asked myself a simple question – What is greater, my goals and dreams or my problems? My goals, without a doubt! The answer was so obvious and powerful that it hit me like a lightning strike. This was a moment of catharsis and the first step to redefining myself. It cleared my dependency from the past and opened new dimensions of life with a much broader vision.

I realized that if I was aiming to reach goals beyond my immediate needs, beyond my comfort zone I needed to explore and adopt new ways of thinking and acting. Remember when you learned how to drive a car and how hesitant you were driving with this silly triangular sign "L" for Learner on the tail of your car?

You already know management is more complicated and demanding than driving a car. The wise and successful leader doesn't hesitate to carry his or her Learner sign, even if he is confident in his capabilities and experience. Being promoted to the next level or running a bigger company changes nothing. It is similar to learning how to drive a larger vehicle. The reason is simple – growing responsibility, complexity, and scale also equals a higher price for every mistake.

Think of a business losing its ability to function effectively and dying slowly as a Code Blue. Code Blue is a phrase used in American hospitals meaning an emergency case with a risk of losing a human life. The same happens with a company that is dying slowly at the hands of its leaders.

There are a number of mistakes we inherit from the past that hold us back, leading to a Code Blue condition for a business. Unfortunately, we tend to drag old mistakes with us like a suitcase with no handle full of dirty laundry. We convince ourselves for too long of its value, even long after we have tired of dragging it around.

I will mention just ten typical mistakes that separate extraordinary leaders from the ordinary.

- Ordinary leaders tend to treat different companies as being similar in nature. However, different organizations have different goals and patterns of resource utilization and so, have different qualities, optimal structures, and assumed properties. All businesses must be treated differently according to their nature and archetype. Treating every business as similar is the simplest way to neglect what makes a given business unique and give up any advantages in its market.

- I have met many owners and directors in my life and found that a majority of them have a lack of vision, and even the concept of vision. Leaders without vision are blind in terms of value creation. They don't want to hear any feedback from employees or customers because where they want to be is unclear even to them. Feedback is valuable for those who know where they are going and every suggestion that keeps them on a track is invaluable.

- An old-fashioned tendency of leaders for patterned, rigid thinking based on old strategies doesn't help to win in modern business battles. This makes one's mind full of dogmas and biases restricting innovation, flexibility, and ultimately disconnects people. Mental rigidity restricts new ideas and innovativeness and limits overall business knowledge even for industry professionals.

- Looking at organizations as nothing more than a collection of individual components results in a blurry picture far different than viewing it as one complete entity. No one can gain control over several disconnected parts each of which behave in their own unpredictable manner. A person feels every limb and part of his body, if not, then something is clearly wrong. In an organization, good leaders must feel every cell of the corporate body in order to care for and build it up. Managing a company as separated functions is like producing knock-off brand clothing. A material seems almost identical to the original; similar buttons, same label, it all looks the same.

However, the fit is horrible, and the overall quality is far from desired, decreasing the price which customers are willing to pay for.

- Leaders are often far too good at creating unnecessary complications and obstacles for their employees and customers. A steady stream of different management fads and fashions makes things even more difficult. It is often called smart, complex thinking. Companies are often managed just for the sake of management while forgetting about employee and customer satisfaction, profit for shareholders, and positive impact on all stakeholders, resulting in a big gap between the desired performance and what is actually happening. A meaningless complication is the enemy of effectiveness and causes chaos and misunderstanding.

- Good leaders attract good employees and help people grow. They connect employees and customers, using positive human emotions and senses. Weak leaders are more likely to destroy people's effort and motivation, making their employees' work and life difficult. They blame everything except themselves, from bad weather, wrong time, or unfavorable positions of the stars. Weak leaders rely on threats to win over people. The sad fact is too many such leaders exist.

- Teams, not crowds, win battles. I found that two out of ten leaders of medium-size companies can define and name their teams clearly, not by functions or departments, but their purposes and goals. Many leaders have little knowledge of their own people and their qualities. Too much effort is needed to get good performance from employees if they are disconnected and do not complement each other. It is no wonder why the best people are leaving. They simple can't find a place where their competencies are utilized.

- Hesitation to learn and adapt to new realities kills chances for spotting opportunities, innovativeness, and as result, limit success. We have memories of such giants as Kodak and Borders. Both used to be on the Fortune 500 list but passed away because they were stuck in the old paradigm of thinking. As Marshall Goldsmith, one of the most influential business thinkers stated: "What got you here won't get you there." A dogmatic way of thinking and acting won't get anyone far in business.

- People prefer dealing with those who share their values and views and understand them. They want to be part of a living process. Unfortunately, many people are caught in negative corporate cultures where invaluable human interaction is artificially replaced by formalities and rules, engagement is penalized by unpaid hard work, loyalty is not valued, and respect is something from another planet. High performance remains only a dream for such companies.

- Fear on the part of leaders to go somewhere unknown is holding many companies back. No one can explore new terrain without accepting risk. Business is a synonym for a risk. The famous nineteenth-century Dutch painter Vincent van Gogh (Vincent Van Gogh, 1937) said, "The fishermen know that the sea is dangerous and the storm is terrible, but they never found these dangers sufficient reason for remaining ashore." There is no success without risk.

You face new rules with every new project. If you notice some of these or even one of these faults, then rush to eradicate them as they will restrict your growth sooner or later.

What will remain important?
Life is changing and people are constantly trying to predict those changes. However, what will remain constant and invariable for years ahead is more important. Whatever is changing is simply

variables that must be considered, but you can't build a solid business around them. Think of the van Gogh quote - the weather and sea are always changing; however, there are four core things that remain the same – a ship, a crew, a captain, and customers waiting for fish.

The same happens in business. The core things remain constant – company, culture, and leadership. These three core elements exist to satisfy customer demand, the fourth and main critical element of the micro eco-system created by any business. A business is strong relative to its weakest element, whether that be leadership, culture, or understanding of the customer.

These four elements form an eco-system that will either successfully fit into a market environment or die if changes are not made.

Organization

I have seen many seemingly successful leaders fail because they failed to understand the nature of their organizations. Rushing to catch up with all the new fads, they forget that an organization is an organic body and treating it as a mechanical unit works against the human nature of the employees and the customers they work to serve.

People can't create anything more clever and complicated than themselves. We are copying ourselves in terms of creating businesses expecting them to grow in a complex environment and achieve harmony within it. This is similar to what we are most familiar with, the human body.

It may sound a little weird to consider a business as an organism, but this allows a leader to grow a company by treating it as a whole and focusing on specific problems at the same time. Such an approach allows more balanced decision-making and scrutinizing assumptions behind innovation, customer service, and growth. A natural and intuitive understanding of an organization allows the creation of seamless and efficient processes which leads to higher performance. Think of a company as the best instrument for satisfying customer needs. You can't do something exceptional if this instrument is sick or broken.

Culture

Corporate culture is the inner energy of an organization formed from the work of employees and their qualities combined to achieve a company's goals. It makes an organization as alive and unique as a human personality. Culture reflects the inner world of the organization and defines how people are cared for, treated, and praised. It gives a human face to the company. The company is efficient and appealing to its employees in terms of active engagement only to the extent it is a natural and comfortable environment.

Culture is multidimensional – it governs the interaction of company members striving to reach the organization's goals; it's the soul of the organizational body. As the dynamic and spiritual core of the organization, it catalyzes personal and organizational development, leading to better performance.

Culture is responsible for the development of people. No company can move further than its employees' competencies. Strategic development is bound by the development of individuals. Mistakes in how people are treated are costlier than any technological or process mistake. A company with a negative culture is falling into an abyss of underperformance without realizing it. It may feel like everything is fine, but the results say different. The underlying cause of underperformance is a cultural bankruptcy. Before anyone recognizes the situation and issues the Code Blue, it is often too late.

These days, corporate culture is essential to competition. This is true for large and small organizations alike. Those with a stronger culture are those who will continue to succeed and grow.

Leadership

Leadership should not rest on past success. Leadership should also not hold onto the past longer than necessary, repeating old mistakes and restricting innovation. Leadership is about having an impact today, and every day, for the sake of creating a bright and attractive future. Leadership is the multidimensional and multi-purposeful function where leaders must have a vision and appropriate capacities to build a future for and with people.

The Emperor of France, Napoleon Bonaparte, said once - "A leader is merely a dealer in hope." (Martyn Lyons, 1994, p. 56) Hope means trusting in something that will happen in the future. People want to see something concrete when a bright future is promised to them – a leader with professionalism and the ability to do a job, expressing care for and understanding of people, and a clear vision of how to get to the future. An effective organization established and managed by a competent leader is an instrument for building this bright future. Culture is envisioned and maintained by the leader and reflects the care and consistent growth of people whose aims and desires are treated as a priority. Culture requires leadership based on vision, inspiration, and exceptional strategic competencies in managing a company, its people, and building customer relationships.

Customer

Customer demand is predictable in that it will continue to change all the time. As customers become more educated and sophisticated their demands will change accordingly.

Relationships between companies and clients can become close, almost a civil partnership. The organization makes an implicit oath to devote all its effort and attention to its customers. Companies match their values with the values of customers aiming to build strong long-lasting relationships. Business involves getting into the era of V2V (values-to-values) relationships.

If a company's focus is shifted away from people, then in time it will be considered by customers (and employees as well) as an unforgivable infidelity. Then everything is lost – all effort, time, hopes, and income.

Please forgive me for such a long letter. I know that you are exceptionally busy. I'll wrap it up with a few more sentences hoping to add more sense to your complicated business journey.

Success is not just given to anyone but earned by those who are brave enough to think boldly and learn every day, aiming to raise their skills from science to art. Modern management must be artful with a leader who is streetwise, book-wise, and nature-wise.

If you want to continue your leadership career, then assume that your main responsibility is care of people and nurturing their qualities and competencies. Devoting all your effort and time into honing your competencies in corporate culture, leadership style, and understanding of customers to an art form is the best investment in your future. It will pay you back in constant personal and professional growth, and simply having more fun doing business.

Take care and be brave,
Me

Chapter One

CORPORATIONS START WITH C FOR CUSTOMERS

What are the chances of selling snow and ice to the dwellers of Greenland? Would you sell a truck of sand to anyone in a desert? Business without customers and their demands is nonsense.

Customers are the alpha and omega of business. Customers need to define the business and provide the means to keep it going. In this sense, the customer is the Emperor of commerce, and his demands must be met and met quickly. If you do so, the Emperor will reward your venture and effort with cash and loyal support. If those orders are ignored, His Majesty the Customer will find another servant - your competitor.

The human demand for any organization's product or service is the main resource for any company. Customer demand reflects how people see what they need and value. The product reflects the business's attempt to meet that demand. A product which reflects the customers' vision and expectations is what matters most in commerce.

Reading customers' minds

Any business begins with the ability to attract this vital resource through a product or service that customers see as valuable. Naturally, this is never done in a vacuum. There are several other organizations in constant competition for the same customers.

An entrepreneur just forming a business or a leader of an established company needs to be a master in hearing customers, a mind reader of sorts. A leader of business must develop this skill to offer extraordinary solutions for customers.

Creators should strive to find ways to engineer solutions for their customers' dreams and their worries. They are creating a future for customers and so, for themselves. They are messengers of the future. They are the ever-curious minds that give meaning to the customers' unspoken desires and needs.

To reach the goal of being an irreplaceable business, the leaders must maintain effective relationships with customers. Yet they must also keep an effective cognitive distance from them. If the cognitive distance is too short, the leader will lose his critical understanding of people. This is like a situation with teenage kids who are very dependent on their parents but don't realize it. Just like a child, the customer who is too close often doesn't fully appreciate their situation.

Too much distance is a danger as well. If the cognitive distance is too long, then businesses and customers won't hear and understand each other. The messages from both sides will amount to nothing more than white noise. This is like watching an advertisement in an unknown language – at best it is humorous, at worst frustrating, always little more than gibberish.

We need to maintain a fellowship with customers. Not a purely transactional relationship, but fellowship. Fellowship - because business and customers should add value to each other in different ways, as old friends. Such relationships are based on mutual affection and support, vision, inspiration, and passion.

Envisioning customer needs

Building something from nothing is not the right way to go about satisfying customers. Leaders (or creators) make great things out of their sophisticated vision of the customer's needs. Vision beyond the conventional thinking and making customers in the center of attention is the path to success.

Envisioning customers' needs is an art unto itself. Ferdinand Anton Ernst "Ferry" Porsche, the true founder of Porsche, envisioned a demand for sports cars in Germany which was only just recovering from ruins after the Second World War. He said - "In the beginning, I looked around and could not find quite the car I dreamed of. So I decided to build it myself." His vision and courageous thinking have since grown into an icon of the automotive industry admired for decades across the globe.

Real creators can see problems in the same light as their customers, but also identify the issues surrounding those problems and so offer new solutions. Modern customers demand multiple solutions to multiple problems in one product. The rise of online learning illustrates this perfectly.

Daniel Alpert and Don Bitzer from the University of Illinois established the very first internet-based community for learning purposes as far back as 1959. A few years later, in 1968, Douglas Englebart along with the Stanford Research Institute crew released the oNLine System program testing the idea of enhancing education via technology. These pioneers envisioned a growing demand for learning and the possibility for many to achieve higher levels of education with ever-improving technology. Since then, millions of people have studied online, and the number is growing every year.

These phenomenal people thought of answers to questions no one was asking yet. The most successful leaders can see not just what is important today, but what will be important tomorrow.

The ability to solve people's problems begins with seeing the world and life from the same perspective, with walking in the customer's shoes. You then act as a guide, offering the shortest and most comfortable route to the offered solutions to the customers' problems.

Greed is often touted as a motivator for business. However, greed is a terrible guide as it gets in the way of a sound customer relationship and stunts long-term vision. No one can equally satisfy both his own greed and the customer's needs. Business is about satisfying and making other people happy while making a profit. Greed is about satisfying oneself only. This divides businesses from the outset between those who are prepared to only run a short distance and those able to run a marathon while building a satisfied and loyal customer base, as in the case of the legendary Porsche.

Passion for customers

A few years ago, I was fly-fishing for salmon on one of those remote ice-cold arctic rivers, Kola, at the far end of Northern Europe. The season had just begun, and the largest fish were swimming in from the sea; aggressive, strong, and enormously beautiful. Early morning, a bit of frost covering everything, the first few proud fins breached the surface. I became focused, channeling my excitement through the fishing rod. Just a few casts and something big began tugging on the line. A few seconds of fighting to get the living, silver torpedo under control… Bang! My favorite and well tested "Sage" rod snapped. It is a traumatic experience for any fly-fisherman – the fish is lost and a fisherman's best friend, his rod, is in pieces nearly ending the season when it has only just begun.

I promptly sent the rod to Sage for repairs. I even attached a note that I was in danger of losing the whole season. Within ten days I got my rod back fixed and good as new. I called the regional manager in the UK to thank him for the fantastic service, saving my season, and praised him for the incredible rods they build. He appreciated my call and said, "We are all very passionate fly-fishermen, from the store clerk to our CEO. Passion for fishing and passion for our clients is what helps us to build such outstanding rods and make people's experience enjoyable. We know what you feel like losing the rod and did our best for you as a fellow fisherman."

Sincere passion and focused understanding of a customer's needs help business to enter the customer's own vision and become naturally accepted. Unity between a business's and customer's vision is the goal. Passion for customers and what they care about increases the business's understanding and care for them.

Passion added into customer care gets people, customers and employees excited. Mutual excitement opens more potential and opportunity for both. Big ideas are built from and based on shared passion.

Sympathy is not enough. Customers demand empathy. In our social lives we take for granted that our friends and family walk with us. In commerce, a business needs first to cross the distance to the customers in order to walk with them. The business should never assume that the customer will cross that distance.

Customer champions love their customers first and often trust their instincts. They know numbers can't explain everything. Customers love them in return, mirroring the effort of a company in loyalty. I've heard business leaders say that they are lucky to have great customers. This has nothing to do with luck. The quality of customers reflects the effort spent in attracting them and how the organization sees them. If you passionately fight for them and love them, then your customers will be loyal, active, and happy to refer your products or services to their contacts. If one doesn't like customers, then he or she always sees them as greedy, nasty, and not responsive.

Being passionate about a beloved spouse means asking questions almost daily – How do you feel? What worries you? What can I do for you? What plans do you have? The same questions should be asked in relation to customers. Unfortunately, even otherwise good organizations don't think of this.

We absorb and understand things that we listen to carefully, with a full heart. Listen to nature, and you will understand it. Listen to customers, and you will understand them. Listening is the most critical skill in business. Hearing every nuance of what they and their friends need, without trying to convince them that they really want something else. Debating and criticizing customers is a sure way of creating a rift between them and the business, killing the business in the process.

Interaction with customers should be as easy as play, not hard work. If it's work, it means that the business has little understanding of its own customers and treats them as some sort of power leveraging exercise. Being naturally obsessed with customer care and satisfaction is a must. Customers are perceptive and will know when you are faking it.

Too many ifs and buts raised by sceptics who focus on delving into tiny details, only create problems. If all a business does is look for problems that is what they will find. Look for solutions, and they will come. Think big about success creating value for people, making positive changes for them, and improving the quality of their lives.

Your passion should show in the details. Rolex built its reputation based on an attention to detail that is reflected in high quality products, care, and service. The result is quality that has appealed to many generations. This is true passion.

Caring for tomorrow's needs today

Nothing is more predictable than ever changing customer demand. Changes in customer demand drive and shape the world of business.

NOTHING is MORE
PREDICTABLE
THAN EVER CHANGING
CUSTOMER DEMAND

Just a decade ago, banks were worried about the slow growth of credit cards. Today, a contactless card is the norm, and payment with a smartphone is as routine as flying across the globe. Not to mention electric cars, smart watches, and a myriad of other things we are taking increasingly for granted.

Customer demand is always changing. People value time, comfort, quality, and convenience more every day. Every new product offered to them yesterday triggers customers' needs for something new that evolves their demands for tomorrow. They want greater value than yesterday. People always want something better. It's in our nature. In this sense, simply offering a new product doesn't necessarily create value for customers. Business must be customer-wise offering products that offer extra value beyond what is already available.

It is pointless to preach to people, begging them to purchase a product that they don't see as valuable. People must be convinced that this product has long-lasting value for them, that it is worth more to them than the price they pay for it. A good business is a customers' servant, helping them meet their needs and achieve their goals.

Modern life is too fast-paced – the days pass by like a high-speed train. People's thoughts are focused on the future, theirs and their kids'. An ability to predict the customer's needs for tomorrow is a matter of business sustainability and prosperous existence in the long run. Tomorrow's customers must be attracted or grown today.

British Metro Bank first opened its doors in the summer of 2010, becoming the first high street bank to open in the UK in over 100 years. It quickly became the most trusted current account and financial provider by offering excellent service that fulfilled clients' needs. At the same time, Metro Bank considered kids as their future clients and sought to engage them as soon as possible by helping them take their first steps with money. Kids are encouraged to save and count their coins using Magic Money Machines and learn about budgeting with their special financial education program. Certainly, these kids will think of this bank when they need a real account.

If not, then what?

Success begins as soon as you clearly realize the need to be more efficient and realize that is related directly to customer satisfaction. Every failure and success demand to be rethought again and again. Every detail is important. Something missing in the care of customers means failure in the future.

Let's imagine an old mentor explaining to his mentee why some companies live long and successful lives while others become nothing more than memories. For instance, the difference between the *Titanic* and *The Queen Elizabeth 2* (*QE2*), two of the most famous passenger ships of the twentieth century. *Titanic* sank on her maiden voyage in 1912 taking 1,500 lives to a watery grave. *QE2* sailed for almost forty years, from 1969 to 2008, proudly taking people across the Atlantic in luxury.

The *Titanic* was considered first as a luxury vessel. Safety was taken for granted. *QE2* by contrast was synonymous with comfort and safety. The difference might seem minor. In the case of the *Titanic*, it is an offering of luxury and comfort, while *QE2* is an offering of luxury with an emphasizing on caring of the human lives. A seemingly minor issue, care through customer safety, can have a dramatic effect on whether the endeavor ends in success or disaster.

Has anything changed in the century since the *Titanic* sank? The Morandi viaduct in Genoa (Italy) collapsed taking 44 lives with it on the August 15, 2018. This tragedy showed that local authorities paid more attention to cars that ride on a bridge rather than to the solidity of that bridge, and its safety. They shifted their focus from people and failed in a tragic fashion.

Co-evolving with customer demand

Customer demand is always changing, and so business should change and evolve accordingly. Peter Drucker (1973, p. 350) stated that "Inside and outside the business enterprise there is constant irreversible change; indeed, the business enterprise exists as the agent of change in an industrial society, and it must be capable both of purposeful evolution to adapt to new conditions and of purposeful innovation to change the conditions."

Ask existing or potential customers – would they invest in your company's shares? If yes, they believe in you and are prepared to take a chance on you. If the answer is no, then your business stands too far from customers making them leery of trusting you in the long run. The reason behind a negative response is simple – the business has fallen out of touch with changing customer demand. Proactive responsiveness and tuning to those changes depend on business coherence when all elements and units of a business are in synergy to satisfy customers.

A business that can't define clearly its own customers loses itself in the debris of adjoining markets and acts like a lunatic without any profit either for itself or its customers. Its products miss targeted customers, and thus the business is effectively invisible.

The aim is not to be better than your competitors, but to attract and keep customers. Stay focused on them and satisfy their needs. This is how you will stand out.

Customer demands and requirements define market niches and the resources available. Such market niches are battlefields for a business where it fights over customers with competitors. Everyone fights for more customers and so, a bigger and more favorable market niche. Those who know their customers best are always in a superior position.

Getting to know customers and their needs demands a lot of legwork, questioning people on what is important for them, and thoroughly analyzing their responses. Talk to senior people for experience and wisdom; talk to young people to learn about their desires and needs which will form upcoming trends; talk to peers to see what is missing now and identify gaps in the market.

Conclusion

How to instill passion for customers into professional care and meaningful actions? In other words, what elements of business remain most critical for expressing a passion and love for customers? Talking about care is nothing unless it is offered professionally, with consistent quality, and in a manner convenient for the customers.

There are three critical pillars of any business that define the ability to satisfy customers – organization, culture, and leadership. These three elements and how they work together define the strength of relationships with customers and their level of satisfaction.

The main aim of a business is to build a caring eco-system where business and customers are called "us." Together they should say "we" representing a tribe, helping each other to grow while maintaining their own identity.

Let's talk in the following chapters about how to build these critical elements into effective eco-systems based on the context and specifics of different types of businesses, of corporate culture, and leadership.

Part One

ORGANIZATION

One may say that it would be logical to begin a discussion of business starting from leadership as a function assigned to the leaders as the creators and developers of a business venture. However, I decided to talk about organizations first for a simple reason. A business represents a trinity consisting of the organization, its culture, and its leadership, none of which can exist without the other.

An organization or company is a bridge linking an entrepreneur and customers, and an instrument for producing the goods and services demanded by the customer. In a sense, an organization is a living body, and as such has certain social responsibilities beyond simply satisfying customer needs.

Customers don't know the names of owners and directors but rather the names of companies they are dealing with. Customers will form their impression of the company based on interactions with employees. These front-line employees will determine whether a customer enters a long-term relationship with a company or move on.

If a leader has an incorrect understanding of what his organization is, what archetype best fits his particular type of business, its properties and potentials, it is bound to fail. Without the organization, a leader is just a general without an army.

Chapter Two

ORGANIZATIONAL SELF-AWARENESS

A happy and strong person has an inner harmony between his or herself and the external world, a mature mind, strong character ready for challenges, and sees the beauty in the world.

I asked experts in psychotherapy to describe a typical patient. Often, they begin as unhappy people with no self-awareness, no real identity. The unhappy person has no willpower to keep things going in the right direction and doesn't see his own value. Such a person sees only problems everywhere, whether in family life or work. Family issues drive an initially happy marriage to regular scandals leading to a painful divorce. Children will often not give such parents any respect. Problems at work make one feel like a victim of bad circumstances without any light at the end of the tunnel. Friends disappear without saying goodbye. Chances for improvement are seemingly non-existent.

In the organizational context, self-awareness can be described as an inner harmony allowing engagement between the organization's core and the external world. Self-awareness defines how successful an organization is in consistently utilizing and adapting its innate qualities to satisfy its customers.

In 2018, the capitalization of the English football club "Manchester United" hit a record high of $4.8 billion despite a long series of losses in important games. The market appreciated its consistent confidence and persistence in satisfying fans and supporters. Successful companies, like Manchester United, understand themselves, their own specific nature, and inner potentials. They make employees and customers satisfied and happy. They act at a higher level and encourage others to do the same. They know well what they are worth, exude confidence and courage, which earns them respect in the marketplace. A successful organisation needs self-awareness as a bird needs strong wings.

An unsuccessful company doesn't believe in itself, often believing that its problems are greater than its capabilities, and thus it isn't responsible for solving them. Those companies imprisoned by organizational depression will not get far. Their doubt is like a mental poison making them powerless and blind to their own potential.

I've had experience with very successful business ventures and some ventures that I would prefer to keep my mouth shut about because they were failures. Failure is painful because it is personal and always tremendous. What kind of pain did I experience after failure? The pain comes not just from failure but realizing that I didn't take full advantage of the potential that was there.

Understanding organization

I've heard many times, and surely you have as well, young people say something like – "My boss is an idiot. I could do so much better." However, people overestimating their abilities and making a bunch of unfounded assumptions has killed many businesses.

According to the Dunning-Kruger effect, the less we know about something the more likely we assume we know a lot about it. This is incredibly common – considering yourself as an expert when you really know very little. In truth, we can study something for a hundred years and still know very little. This is the case with our knowledge of human anatomy. Our understanding of organizational anatomy is no different. Organizations and their nature are so complex that there is always something to learn. By looking differently at aspects of an organization that seem familiar we will always find something new if we are prepared to learn.

ORGANIZATIONS AND their NATURE ARE SO COMPLEX that there is always something to LEARN

Any organization is multidimensional and the more dimensions and properties we understand and know how to use, the greater our advantage in the marketplace. Leading a business successfully means giving a company power by understanding its true nature and growing in the right direction. Effort is important but in what direction it is applied makes a difference. Your effort should be focused towards a specific goal determined by your level of understanding.

To map unexplored potentials and hidden reserves one should walk around an organization gazing, not glancing, at every critical part of it, aiming to understand it the way you would try to understand someone you love.

Success depends on performance. In turn, organizational performance is bound by the superiority of our understanding of properties, functions, and their interdependency. The more we understand the organization, the more effective it will be and the more profit we will earn for shareholders, employees, and stakeholders.

It may sound strange, but many leaders and managers tend to forget that an organization's main purpose, especially in commerce, is to earn a profit for its owners. We simply forget about this critical purpose being bogged down in the day-to-day routine. As a result, many businesses lose focus and don't explore the full potential of their companies.

Six properties

Customers are gatekeepers of demand and money. To win their support a company must exploit all its potentials. This means developing six properties – being a living body, being a strong interface between itself and customers, being a mini marketplace, standing out from the competition, and being an essential part of the relevant market.

customers are GATEKEEPERS Of demand and money

Living body

Any organization is alive, much like a human or any other creature. Any company is formed by people to serve people. Organizations should be seen as living entities that can be taught to breathe, function, move, and develop inside their specific environments. We give them proud names believing in their great destiny and care for them much like we do for our children.

An organization is not merely a combination of hard and soft systems, but a living body. Similar to people, organizations also suffer from diseases and pathologies that need to be categorized in order to select the appropriate treatment.

For millennia, famous strategists and tacticians such as Sun Tzu, Julius Caesar, Alexander the Great, Napoleon, Nelson, and Genghis Khan viewed their armies as a single living body, placing emphasis on developing a sense of belonging and integration amongst their people with success or failure being communally shared. Refusal to support other regiments was heavily penalized, and thus they were able to develop powerful armies which were maneuverable, strong and controllable. Corporations or organizations are cohesive wholes too, not merely collections of individuals and processes.

We create organizations in part by copying ourselves and the natural processes around us. Organizations are created by humans and reflect the nature of their creators and are fairly similar to human beings in several ways. Looking at any organization we can envision the roles and functions as organs, limbs, muscles, brain functions, senses, nervous systems, circulatory systems, and digestion.

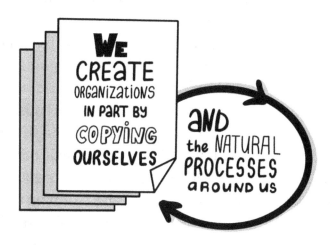

We CREATE ORGANIZATIONS IN PART BY COPYING OURSELVES AND the NATURAL PROCESSES AROUND US

An organization has a skeleton of a certain type. It has complex central and peripheral nervous systems, and organs with specific functions responsible for the transformation and transmission of resources. The skeleton depends on the type and pattern of its processes and the resources utilized by each organization that makes them different. The brain of the organization exists in the physical map of its governance structure - the board of directors and management structure are responsible for the coordination of all internal processes and the development of external relationships as well as developing the organization as a strong and resourceful entity. Functional departments are not single and independent units but valuable and vital parts of the eternal process of resource transformation, which must be designed to produce the best organizational potentials and secure successful development.

Organizations often have different functional disorders, whether imprinted from the moment of establishment or developed during their life, which directly influences their performance. Thus, we need to understand it as a whole where an internal problem in one part of the body causes malfunctions in other parts as well. Failure to understand this would be like taking a ride through a storm on a ship with a faulty navigation system, malfunctioning engine, and without means of communication. Not many people would volunteer to be involved in such an extreme situation.

The human body is developed to be able to survive in different conditions and environments through adaptation to local conditions. Similarly, organizations are built for survival and profit-making in different environments and conditions, i.e., countries, markets, and industries.

A means of serving customers

The foremost purpose of any organization is to cultivate happy customers, today and in the future. No organization exists for itself, it will always be customer-dependent. An organization is a means or instrument of producing a product or service and delivering it in a form and fashion demanded by customers.

An organization is a body born to act for customers, with a particular purpose, and in particular conditions. Its strength grows not because of investments into it or the number of people working for it, but because of its ability to serve a consistently growing number of customers by satisfying their evolving demands, offering great care, and responding to ever-changing needs.

If a company's customer base is not growing then no amount of investment or stock options can save it. For instance, GoPro, the company that produces quality portable cameras was valuated at $13 billion in 2015. All seemed okay and then... three years later, in 2018, the company was valued at $900 million putting it on the brink of bankruptcy. The company hasn't been able to reach more customers and grow sales because its cameras are no longer better than those made by Garmin or other competitors. GoPro had failed to offer appropriate service, exploit all potentials, and diversify its product since the beginning in 2002.

Stakeholders, customers, and investors are ultimately looking for a long-term relationship with a company, not the equivalent of a one-night stand. That means offering a look into the company's history, its present workings, and plans to improve the relationship in the future.

Customers believe in a product if they know that a strong and fully capable company stands behind it. The product can't be a one-off and needs to be fully supported for an extended length of time. People want to see clear evidence that the company is growing in understanding of their needs and capacity to fulfill them. Understanding an organizations' importance is natural for people as we are customers or members of different organizations throughout our lives – school, hospitals, university, army, workplace, airlines, etc. Customers only join or support these organizations if they believe in them.

Living interface

An organization is a living interface between its owners and leaders and its customers. Employees are like an organic bridge connecting businesses and customers. Organizations consist of people permanently interacting with internal and external stakeholders. Organizations and people as customers become involved in sustaining the life of a company. These interlinked processes need to be understood as dynamic, continuously operating parts of a living organism.

For instance, when the police officer stops you, you think of that officer as part of the Police Department as an organization and call to mind what it stands for. As customers (or citizens), we interact with this officer as a representative of the Police Department that enforces a country's laws and regulations meant to serve and protect us.

An organization is a means of communicating the leaders' vision of how customers should be treated, and how employees understand it. Once mistreated, we as customers think of its leaders and their organization as someone assaulting us personally. While communicating with the organization we assume poor service is the result of employees being instructed to treat people poorly. This is partially true. Bad employees are often the result of bad leadership.

Being an interface between leaders and customers, the organization shows its responsiveness to different demands and needs, striving to meet even those that go beyond ordinary expectations. At the same time, this interface allows customers to tell businesses about themselves and so, is very effective if a business is prepared to listen and improve where needed.

If not, then it is like a broken vending machine which neither gives coffee nor returns the money. In real life, customers stop dealing with the entire organization (vending machine) and not just one part of it (drink selection button) and walk away.

Internal marketplace

An organization is like a mini marketplace. The employees spend much of their time offering their effort and skill to the organization, customers, and their fellow employees. The effective organization inspires employees into an effective workforce meant to serve customer needs.

In a broad sense, an organization is a place where people think of others, care and act for them while gaining a profit for themselves. In short, we profit best by seeking to serve others first.

In return for their employees' efforts, the organization transforms people by educating, training, enhancing professionalism, securing income and care, and having a social impact on employees and their families and society at large.

The organization is a place for professional and personal growth. The relationships between organizations and employees also resemble a credit agreement. Employees lend their competencies and qualities to the organization expecting a return in the form of professional growth.

Employees are internal clients of an organization. They are carriers and holders of professional resources and rightfully want their resources to grow. Fair pay is a basic norm but not sufficient for maintaining strong relationships between organizations and employees. People expect and deserve more than mere income. Money alone is not the main draw for great employees anymore.

Look at the young generations. They want interesting tasks that allow them to grow and exercise their creativity by working together with interesting people. They want to be part of something great while being valuable to society and have a direct impact on the future.

No one can grow being isolated, and people realize this. People are collective creatures and come to organizations naturally expecting to be among colleagues and rivals who will help them grow. The organization represents a place of active interaction between employees similar to a family. They expect a shared language and values. The leaders are obliged to make it comfortable, attractive, and full of energy, and help people to act as one strong body.

Different traits and types

Organizations are different in their nature. Different organizations are created with a different purpose and thus grow differently from their moment of birth.

Likewise, people are different in their physical types, ethnicity, age, and day to day social practices, organizations differ in a number of obvious ways as well. Besides being different in size, operational principles, and age, organizations are different in their dedication to serving particular customers' needs, and how they acquire and utilize internal and external resources. Different organizations have different idiosyncratic attributes where if something is good for one type of organization it can be deadly for another type.

Can any bank survive on two percent annual profit as airlines do? Would a furniture producer or carmaker survive using the same business model as a hotel? What are the differences in resources between a university and a charity?

How can we make sense of this? There are five groups or archetypes of organizations that can be identified based on organizational taxonomy. This is similar to taxonomy in the biological sciences, i.e., the classification of biological creatures developed by Carl Linnaeus in the second part of the eighteenth century. He grouped different species based upon shared physical characteristics and specific properties looking beyond their most obvious differences.

Based on this classification the five archetypes are producers, knowledge-dependent, location-dependent, donor-dependent, and state-affiliated organizations. Besides the difference in visual typology, every archetype has specific features, characteristics, and optimum configurations.

The difference between organizations defines the need for building and managing them and exploring their potentials differently. Organizations achieve superior performance only if we understand their true nature and unleash their full potential. Otherwise, we will continue to expect them to do things they were never meant to do. Stop demanding your dog to fly and your cat to swim long distances. Let them do what they are best at.

ORGANIZATIONS ACHieve SUPeRiOR PERFORMANCE ONlY iF WE UNDeRSTAND their tRUe NATURe AND unleAsh their FUll POTENTiAL

Some companies intuitively understand their true nature, some do not. In a practical way, I can say that one of my clients improved overall effectiveness by 60% within four months just by realizing his company's specific qualities and getting rid of atypical properties.

An organization's typology influences the mode of corporate culture and leadership in its specific context. We will look into these five archetypes in greater detail in the following chapter.

Part of a big eco-system, economy

Imagine a country's economy as an ocean which consists of different markets, hidden streams of trends, and inevitable storms that shake it from time to time. Every organization whether large or small is a stream that flows into this ocean.

No company can be viewed as being independent of its main eco-system. Every organization is a part of a local and international market. At the same time, every organization faces different challenges - the rate of growth of competitors; incidents of strong and unfair competition; scarcity of and constraining conditions around resources, whether in terms of human resources, land, commodities; changes to industry and other external standards; and finally, the demand for higher quality of products and services.

The stronger the companies forming a national economy, the stronger the economy will be. A strong economy demands more products and so, more active companies. It is accustomed to input from healthy and strong companies. This leads to a growing economy which stimulates the growth of new companies. This is an eternal circle and every company is an important part of it being responsible for adding value to the economy and society.

Conclusion

The less we know about an organization the fewer chances we have to initiate change and better serve customers. The limits of an organization's effectiveness depend on the organization's self-awareness and leaders' ability to align all properties and sequence them in the most efficient way to maximize the return on investment. The more we know about the organization, the fewer limits we face. By becoming self-aware, an organization is developing and fully exploiting its imprinted strengths and potentials and better serving its customers.

Practical Tips:

- Only a strong and self-aware company can attract great employees, partners, and customers. Confidence, a strong mental state, and motivation for growth are what attract people.

- Giving up on the organization by not treating it properly is like surrendering your arms to an enemy at the beginning of a battle. What is the chance of victory for a weaponless warrior?

- Show me what you do in developing all sides and properties of the organization, not in words, but in actions and results. Advertising this will draw in more customers.

- There are no miracles in this sense as a focus on money doesn't pay back. An organization is profitable only if it serves customers.

Chapter Three

A BUSINESS DNA: A TYPOLOGY OF ORGANIZATIONS

Every time I speak or lecture, I am asked how to get the most out of a company. In my view, a company is a masterpiece when it acts at 100% of its potential every day. If 30-40% of its capacity is wasted today, then it can't be recovered tomorrow. This means a company is losing ground to competitors because of an insufficient understanding of its own nature. We don't start companies with the intent of operating at half strength, but the reality is that this happens far too often.

A clear understanding of the organization's nature helps keep one focused on its core purpose, keeping it on the right path. Being focused also requires removing all distractions. If a person is focused, he is many times more productive. The same happens with organizations. An unfocused business lurches from one direction to the next, never solving any real problems, and leading to fatigue as they pile up. The constant turmoil that results leaves no room or energy for creative innovation.

Do all companies have similar DNA? Different organizations have different imprinted DNA which influences their way of conducting business and serving customers. Organizations are nestled in different archetypes which group them by similarity according to how they interact with customers, patterns of internal and external resource utilization, mode of organizational relationships, optimum configuration of functions, and where core resources are located – internally or externally.

There are five archetypes of organizations – producers, knowledge-dependent, location-dependent, donor-dependent, and state-affiliated organizations. I first presented this typology of organizations in *Organisational Anatomy* (Konovalov, 2016), and part of this chapter will echo that work.

ORGANIZATIONAL ARCHETYPES

Clarity concerning an organizations' nature will help to keep the "company = customer" equation balanced every day. The clear picture gives us faith in the future and gives us power today. It motivates us for immediate and effective actions.

Simplicity and clarity beat chaos. Problems, issues, misunderstandings, misbehavior, and misconduct of employees are actually indicators of chaos. Chaos is not fertile soil for organizational growth and success. The greater problems we face, the more simplicity and clarity we demand in understanding the organizations we work or partner with. An understanding of archetypes helps one gain a holistic picture and helps navigate a company to success.

Let's take a journey across archetypes, different planes of business reality where each one has its own rules of engaging customers and peculiarities of conducting business.

Producers

The world of producers is fascinating, noisy, and fast moving. It is a world of those who always keep their hands busy and stay on their toes looking for new ways to do things.

People need food, clothing, houses, books, furniture, and millions of other things. They appreciate producers for what they do for us and their effort in making things better and better. Producers magically transform different materials into something useful for people. Actually, any organization where the core activity lies in the transformation of inbound materials can be classified as a producer. They may be carmakers, shipbuilders, winemakers, fish curers, builders, meat processors, pharmaceutical companies or in other words, anyone who transforms external resources and adds value to them, whether they will be turned into a ready-to-use product or semi-product.

Considering the rapid expansion of different tech companies, we should not forget about producers of software, applications, platforms, and other content. Think of Microsoft, Facebook, Netflix, YouTube, and even your friends' small start-up creating online games, as they are producers of different sorts. We need their products for exploring and enjoying the virtual part of the modern world. These companies form a sub-archetype of tech producers. Modern life can't be imagined without their products.

Also, a shift towards digital technologies has dramatically changed the world of producers. Specifically those high-tech companies where there have been many high profile winners and losers. For instance, Nokia, a former leader in mobile phones, lost for several reasons, the most critical being not recognizing the shift from product-based to platform- and application-based competition.

Producers are the bridge between supply and demand. Producers depend on the quality of inbound resources, their internal expertise, and their ability to satisfy customer demand. They are dependent on the quality of their supply chain and that quality is in the final product.

Imagine a fish processor who demands a stable supply of fish of a certain standard and within a certain price range. Without that reliability, he either couldn't meet demand or costs would be astronomical, or both. In order to secure a stable supply of their core resource, the fish processor must establish strong and robust relations with suppliers, whether local or abroad. At the same time, the fish processor must know exactly what his consumers require and meet their expectations.

While you read this book think of a publisher as a producer. Their inbound material is a manuscript produced by an author who has taken his thoughts and run them through many developmental stages before converting them into a book. Publishers are producers of such intellectual properties and are required to be experts in evaluating that intellectual material, understanding the market and adding value to it. I know of brilliant books that did not have good sales because of the publishers' incompetence as a producer. There are also many bad books that lead to a loss for publishers because they didn't properly evaluate the initial manuscript.

However, for producers, it is important to not only produce a product and sell it but to provide appropriate services and aftersales care which reflects the effort placed into development and production of the product. This issue is very critical for them and may significantly influence brand perception.

A producer's quality is also reflected in the ability to provide exceptional sales, after-sales care, and regular upgrades, particularly for technically complicated products like cars, electronics, and software. After-sales service extends the life of a product making it more profitable for a customer. Otherwise, an unserved product will have a short lifespan with little value for customers. Few would purchase a car or washing machine that would be impossible to repair.

We can't imagine a producer without appropriate facilities as well as reliable, affordable, and advanced equipment. For instance, before building a start-up, funds must be invested in production with any return to be made within a short while. This creates a lot of risk for investors and demands corresponding effort from the leadership.

Customers expect to see a balance between the declared level of quality, price, a product's innovativeness or uniqueness, sales, and after-sales service. Goods or services are expected to be unique to some extent, whether it is in the design, functionality, or quality. To reach this balance, producers must develop strong relations with all relevant industry actors to stay on top.

To stay abreast of contemporary trends and the competition, producers must also invest in research and development to adopt and develop new technologies. Failure to do so opens up the market to competitors who can manage this 'arms race' more successfully. Some get so far behind that they can never recover.

These technology mavens spread their products and engage customers through a network of dealers and retailers. No one sells at the factory gate. Instead, a strong distribution network is required. Working to create inventory is suicidal for producers. It doesn't matter how great a product is if it can't move its products as widely as possible. Producers are only as good and strong as their technology and distribution capacity.

Knowledge-dependent organizations

Knowledge-dependent organizations represent an incredible world that is never in a rush and very dynamic at the same time. They know their value and importance and prefer to think over questions again and again. Customers need them for their ability to think beyond the boundaries of conventional logic, and help in specific areas such as healthcare, education, finance, or any other expertise.

Knowledge-based organizations generate and exploit knowledge as a product turning it into a currency used for wellbeing, personal and professional growth. They rely on their own expertise and external demand for them to produce intangible goods and services. People demand their specific expertise in healthcare, education, banking and finance, coaching and training, and different forms of consulting.

They grow as their organizational expertise increases which allows them to attract more customers. For instance, in the bank scenario, money is being made using expertise in financing. A hospital relies on the expertise of its doctors. An accountant may not need much tangible equipment but relies on his/her knowledge of how to report the accounting figures accurately. They must also be fully aware of all the latest regulatory changes. We choose a college, university, or business school by looking at rankings based on the level of knowledge and expertise developed inside the entity and its ability to teach students. Other examples of experts include high-class restaurants which rely on expertise in cooking and gourmands who will travel for delicious food and a memorable evening.

Knowledge-dependent organizations profit from utilizing and capitalizing on knowledge and their internal resources. Expertise in growing inner knowledge and an ability to present it to customers is their main concern as it allows for attracting new customers and outfighting competitors. Inner knowledge makes them independent to some extent from outside partners unless it's necessary for acquiring more knowledge. Managing knowledge-dependent organizations means managing knowledge and the people who generate it.

Brand recognition also plays a significant role. Banks and insurance companies place their advertisements widely in a city, on TV, or at sports events, whereas clinics run special public programs and free no-obligation health checks, and consultants offer free seminars to attract new customers. They also offer differentiated service packages to attract new customers. However, what happens in reality after the 'signing on the bottom line' is often completely different from the promotional material, revealing a much lower level of competence than advertised.

The external relationships between knowledge-dependent organizations and their customers are often not as long-lasting as claimed. Who would remember that you haven't been a bank's client for many years once you have closed an account? What is the strength of the relationships between the university and its graduates other than contacts asking for donations or internship provision?

However, these organizations still need some externally generated, high-value resources. For instance, hospitals need X-ray equipment or expensive tomography services; banks need sophisticated computer systems; universities need to fill their laboratories with appropriate equipment, and so on. Such equipment or services are purchased intermittently, and the equipment has a support function in increasing the worth of the organization. Thus, their relationships with suppliers are usually short-term or project-bounded.

Metaphorically speaking, the knowledge-dependent organization is Master Yoda – wise and having influence far greater than its size. We may not notice the role of knowledge-dependent organizations in economic growth, thinking more of the producers as the ones who add value into the market. However, a population's level of education is directly related to its economic growth. Countries such as South Korea, Sweden, Singapore, Germany, Switzerland, Japan, Finland, USA, and the UK have both some of the best education systems and strongest economies in the world.

Unfortunately, intelligence does not equal infallibility. Significant problems arise when these organizations stop valuing their main resource – people who generate or analyze knowledge. For instance, I have seen universities that treat administrative staff as more important than professors and lecturers. They are simply giving up their main asset while blaming competition for their failures.

Regrettably, quite often knowledge-dependent organizations shift focus from offering knowledge and expertise to offering services. Immediately, such companies fall into patterned thinking, uniformity of activities, and copying competitors. We can often see this in banks, for instance, which instead of focusing on money management behave as service operators or even controllers of customers' assets.

Also, universities, hospitals, sports clubs, and other knowledge-dependent organizations often go bankrupt because they don't understand their own costs and internal structures.

Location-dependent organizations

The aim of location-dependent organizations is to bring their service or product to the largest number of people possible. Their key asset is simple – location. Business and other organizations that rely on this model include resorts, shops, coffee shops, fast-food, telecom, libraries, airlines, postal service, shipping companies, and many other services.

A difference in location means a difference in not just the customer base, but often the specific needs and wants of the customers. The successful location-dependent organization always keeps customers in mind, considering special demands and needs, age, purchasing potential, and the behavioural patterns of local social groups.

What is the difference between shops? Are there dramatic differences for customers buying food at similar supermarkets? Possibly not in the amount of money spent, level of service, and products - the key difference is location. The location matters to the customers and for the retailer's logistics. People choose what is most convenient for them and easy to reach. If a shop or a coffee place is as little as fifty meters away from a shopping or walking route, foot traffic will be poor.

When two or more retailers are located within the same area, we can observe the competition between them through local price benchmarking, discounts, or other matching offers. With a huge array of similar products, competition is about the level of service and "competition of discounts." The winner is the organization that can offer something more and better, but still within the optimal location for customers.

A five-star hotel is unlikely to thrive in a depressed area or on the outskirts of a city. For these organizations, the location must be safe, pleasant, convenient, and even exotic in some cases for resorts, hotels and golf clubs, or very safe and convenient for shops and other services. Before opening a new business, one should learn as much as possible about a location and its potentials, such as other organizations and opportunities in the area; a famous opera house, historical place, or simply an excellent spot to watch an incredible sunset.

We often think about airlines, transport services, telecommunications companies, and broadband providers as kinds of producers, but they are not. They are directly dependent on assigned areas in which they can conduct their business. Their coverage area grows when the organizations grow bigger - for instance, an airline adding new routes into its portfolio.

All of us pay monthly bills for electricity, water, and gas. These are location-dependent companies as well. They buy resources from producers and act as distributors to sell them to us.

Location is a premium for many more companies than we commonly imagine. A couple of years ago, one of my former students established a business placing advertising posters on special platforms fitted on the vans parked around of one of the big

European cities. The business was okay but not growing much. I asked him what he was selling. He responded – Advertisement. I said – "No. You are selling a visible location. You are a location-dependent company. You are helping your clients to attract the attention of as many people as possible. Your value is not in vans but in a place where more people will see the posters." Just two days later he wrote to me that he changed the approach and the offer and enjoyed an immediate response from customers with a doubled number of requests.

Thanks to modern technologies, location-dependent organizations can offer a broad range of online services. Today, an organization's online services can reach a whole world. Think of such giants as Amazon, Alibaba, Uber, and Airbnb. They are growing bigger and bigger every day.

A serious problem for large traditional and online location-dependent organizations is falling out of touch with customers. Far too often these companies focus on maintaining strong relationships with those who secure the appropriate plot of land or signing licenses and permissions while forgetting about customers.

They have a long list of potential suppliers and will not invest in these relationships as it is very easy to change or replace the supplier or remove a brand from a shelf unless the product offered is unique or the payment terms are extremely favorable to the retailer. They begin to act like untouchable oligarchs.

However, not meeting customer demand leads to significant drops in business, often very quickly. For instance, the UK retail giant, Tesco, faced an embarrassing retreat from the American market losing nearly $1.5 billion in 2012. Tesco focused on offering typical British ready meals to US customers and drastically failed.

Donor-dependent organizations

Supporting and giving to others is a great quality of human beings allowing people to live beyond purely selfish interests.

We all owe some part of ourselves to others, to the world we grow up in and giving back to it is an obligation. Helping others gives us a sense of satisfaction, social value, and supports those in great need. Today, we think of a global citizenship seriously helping people in their own countries and abroad as the norm.

Another archetype of organizations is completely dependent on the generosity of others. These donor-dependent organizations include charities, Non-Governmental Organizations (NGOs), different voluntary funds, Faith-Based Organizations (FBOs), and political parties. These organizations attract donors by using an emotional attachment or human willingness to sacrifice something towards a goal or purpose to ensure their survival.

Donor-dependent organizations are dealers in kindness, support, and belief. Knowledge of people is their primary asset. They have two groups of customers, i.e., two focal resources – donors and recipients. They must serve both groups with great care and attention and be capable of building strong relationships with both. In this sense, they must be masters of social capital.

They should understand and feel people's pain, worries, and desires, and help professionally. Charities help people in need, easing conflicts and the consequences of disasters, getting donations from those thinking beyond themselves. Religious organizations serve God and their congregations. Political parties aim to serve and develop society, represent the interests of their voters and get support and donations from their members and supporters.

We can see a number of online donor-dependent organizations grow on a daily basis; different online fundraisers, missionaries, support groups or organizations helping people to combat depression, home violence, and other problems. Online services help donor-dependent organizations spread their influence wide and let a society know about their activities.

Donor-dependent organizations need to fulfill an administrative budget and meet the requirements of their mission statements, such as charitable aims, political goals, or other altruistic purposes. To do this, they need to maximize resources through donations or other resource contributions, such as professional skills or volunteering. They need a steady flow of donations from a greater possible number of sources. In their view, it is better to receive a small but regular donation for years to come than receive a single large donation.

However, the willingness and ability to donate are related to moral and ethical views. Donor-dependent organizations must be highly skilled at after-sales service to solicit repeat donations from 'warm donors', which are critical to their survival while recruiting new donors. Relationships with donors require investment to remain strong and long-lasting to ensure continued long-term support.

Problems arise when a donor-dependent organization focuses on only one group of customers, either recipients or donors, or even worse, on the organization itself. Then they can't fulfill their role of being the distributors of kindness and lose their support base as a result. Willingness to donate is a voluntary act of social reciprocity.

Who will support a religious organization that doesn't take care of its parishioners? Who will donate to a charity that can't take care of hurricane victims professionally and efficiently? Who will support a political party that doesn't stand for supporters or fulfill its promises?

The logic is simple. If a religious organization doesn't take care of parishioners, then people rightfully believe that it can't serve God respectfully either. If a charity can't use the entrusted funds effectively, then people won't see a reason to waste money on amateurs. If a political party will take care only of itself and members and supporters, the next election will be costly.

State-affiliated organizations

State and state-affiliated organizations encompass those responsible for our defense, security, justice, development, general education, infrastructure development, and many other functions related to running a country.

State-affiliated organizations include government departments, agencies, para-state entities, etc. Also, other innovations that have triggered the development of different online services and state-affiliated organizations are not an exception, whether for passport services, cybersecurity, or communal services.

It is impossible to find an ideal country, city, or town on Earth where each state-affiliated organization has only minor problems. A state is a huge and extremely complicated organization and management of it is an extreme and mind-blowing task. They try to reconcile different interests and address urgent and distant necessities within the confines of an uncertain budget.

That budget also needs to be spent before the next budget period. Often, governmental accounting practices lead to abrupt changes in decision-making strategies around the financial year, particularly towards the end of it. At the same time, being bound by a budget, they often face situations that can't be predicted. In August 2005, for example, Hurricane Katrina took more than 1,500 lives in the New Orleans area, left thousands of people homeless, and caused $105 billion in damage. The storm lasted only a few days, but the restoration of damages has taken years even with support from the US government, international response, and many volunteers.

However, since they are the arms of the state, these organizations are not subject to the same level of accountability as organizations belonging to the other archetypes which are often heavily regulated to prevent fraud or money laundering. They enjoy a privileged position to some extent, enjoying almost unlimited access to resources.

There is low or very limited responsibility for their performance and often no sanctions if performance is poor. This lack of accountability also gives rise to the low transparency of management's decision-making and high inertia as they are limited in their willingness to change. Public scrutiny can also translate into political agendas regarding staffing levels, meaning efficiencies may be lost.

The most critical purposes of state-affiliated organizations, in all countries, are the provision and care of all necessary conditions for the development and flourishing of organizations of the four other archetypes; secure and comfortable living of citizens, and enhanced value of state assets.

Unfortunately, state managers far too often focus purely on budget, simply forgetting about these critical goals. They must remember that their achievements are weighed in the court of public opinion.

Problems come when the state treats millions of citizens as one customer and adopts one way of interacting with them all, not considering other organizations as equals. It may sound strange, but it happens more often than we think.

Far too often, government and state-affiliated organizations in every country write off huge amounts of poorly managed money or treat contractors inappropriately. For instance, the National Health Service (NHS) in the United Kingdom a few years ago abandoned its massive new computer system losing $16 billion at the cost of taxpayers.

Conclusion

In modern commerce, many businesses have shifted their main focus from production to branding, public relations, image building, and other activities which fail to enhance the business. They tend to lose their ability to create value at the cost of creating an inflated but false image of positivity and credibility. Customers need a certain product and not an image. Therefore, focusing on the customers' needs pays much better.

A company is more flexible when properly defined rather than trying to be something it's not. Any organization is best served by working within its archetype rather than trying to force itself into another. Ultimately, this leads to a complete lack of purpose that is felt from the top of the organization to the bottom. Knowing and understanding the properties of one's own organizational archetype helps the company to stay on the right path.

As I mentioned before, the evolution of technology has given birth to various sub-archetypes – tech companies. Virtual services will continue to grow in prominence as further technologies develop.

ORGANIZATIONAL ARCHETYPES

Archetypes	Producers	Knowlege-dependent	Location-dependent	Donor-dependent	State and State-affiliated
Traditional	Agriculture, Food producers, Construction, Oil and gas, Furniture, Carmakers, Fishing, Power plants, Clothing, Publishers, etc.	Educacation, Healthcare, hospitals, clinics, Law firms, Research & analytics, Banking, Insurance, High-end restaurants, Consultants, Sport clubs, etc.	Shops, Hotels, Transportation, (airlines, trains, bus, taxi, ferries), Coffee shops, Telecom, Utility services, Estates, Travel agents, etc.	NGOs, Charities, FBOs, Political parties, Social support organizations, Humanitarian initiatives, Public associations, etc.	Public services, Defence, Justice, Police, Regulators, Federal and Local citizens services, etc.
Tech	Software solutions, Platforms & programs (incl. games), Content producers, etc.	Online banking and finance, Remote health screening & checks, Online trainig and education, etc.	Online shops Platforms, Travel bookings, etc.	Online support groups, Online fundraisers, Online missionary, Support centres, etc.	Governmental e-services, etc.

Being in the wrong archetype leads to seven dramatic consequences for an organization:

- Waste of resources. Waste is already one of the biggest problems on our planet;

- Poor understanding of the target audience and not matching business with customers;
- High costs of attracting customers;
- Not valuing the right talent and chasing inappropriate competencies;
- Chasing every trend, leading to exhaustion;
- High transaction and governance costs;
- Infected markets.

In addition to the aforementioned negative consequences, organizations may face different typological pathologies and disorders that drastically harm performance and will be discussed in later chapters.

Practical tips

- Successful strategies can't be built and executed based on poor understanding of an archetype, and its imprinted properties, and unique characteristics. This would be similar to building a stronghold on sand.

- No company can be effective simultaneously in two different archetypes. Even if an umbrella organization runs different businesses, it should keep running them as separate entities. However, many companies are misled into running different businesses with the same model. For instance, a producer may set up a shop; a location-dependent entity. Shops are not producers even when owned by a producing company. An airline corporate training center is a knowledge-dependent branch of a location-dependent company and responsible for generating knowledge, not flying passengers. They can't be run the same way.

- Dare to question every day whether you as a leader have explored every potential of your company and its unique properties. This will help to the evolve organization, its people, and get closer to customers.

- There is no superior archetype. Organizations from different archetypes are interdependent in their existence and influence each other's growth.

- Assigning a company to the wrong archetype causes a mismatch between passion and profit. This is like taking the wrong train. You will reach a destination, but it will be the wrong one. Trying to act in the wrong archetype kills what was a positive environment, leading to being concentrated on numbers only. A healthy and well-defined business creates bigger payoffs to owners, employees, and customers.

- Don't compromise the specific type of your organization for something trendy and short-term. Forcing inappropriate properties and functions onto a company is never rewarding and will be damaging in the long run.

- Develop your employees. This will improve their morale and enhance their creativity and loyalty, unleashing new potential for the company.

- A clear understanding of one's own archetype and its properties makes it easier to diagnose problems and stand strong in the competition for customers. Simplicity always wins over complication and makes it easier to translate decision into action.

Chapter Four

A CHECKLIST OF ESSENTIALS FOR CUSTOMER RELATIONS

A few years back, I witnessed how a successfully growing medium-sized fish company from the UK, Icebrit, suddenly went bankrupt. The company was one of the top sellers of quality frozen white fish, selling fish from its North Atlantic fishing vessels internationally, from Canada to China. Seemingly nothing could undermine its firm position as a well-recognized and reliable supplier.

Icebrit's Managing Director had decided to expand operations to a new location, the North Pacific Ocean. The MD didn't listen to the warnings of the top managers responsible for purchasing and sales. They warned that the North Pacific is very different from the North Atlantic market with its own rules of engagement and expectations. In other words, they warned the MD that such a move would be like going from hunting in the frozen north to the jungle.

If something could go wrong, it did. Everything that the Icebrit's MD was warned about happened. Right after the first two operations in the new market, the company went bankrupt with multimillion-dollar losses. It happened so swiftly that there was little if any chance to do something to save the business. There was no miraculous recovery and many companies and people were seriously harmed.

What went wrong? The answer to this question is more complex than it may seem. Let's look at it step by step. We will use this real case for further discussion of how to analyze corporate actions in order to increase a company's value, get closer to customers, and avoid fatal mistakes.

Every story, every problem always has a lesson if you look at it thoroughly from different angles. Ever-changing conditions, daily problems, unverified trends work against the company, causing inconsistency in performance. A leader must check whether something went wrong or not. To analyze company actions and validate them against being in line with customers' demands we should look at five critical aspects – archetype properties, operational strategies, size limitations, the efficiency of external relations, and efficiency of critical governance processes.

The aim is to determine whether a company is retaining its foundational and authentic properties or has stepped onto risky ground. It is important to note that previous wins are not a guarantee of future success if the company loses an understanding of itself.

Archetype

Practically everyone has experience dealing with recruitment agencies as either a client or candidate. Recruitment agencies appeared about seventy years ago, during WWII, in order to close gaps in the workforce after men were mobilized and demand for able workers was at its peak. They also aided veterans returning home to find employment. Their reputation was excellent at the time.

However, since then, HR agencies have shifted from their initial purpose, jeopardizing reputation at the cost of quick and fat deals. The latest research conducted by "AnyGood?" (UK) in 2018 showed that over 90% of people say they do not trust recruitment agencies, 80% of job hunters are very concerned about where the recruitment sector is heading, 54% believe that they are charging unreasonable fees, and less than 10% trust recruitment agencies to do a good job of matching candidates and roles.

What happened to HR agencies? Fundamentally, they are knowledge-dependent organizations that sell their expertise and knowledge, relying in part on the strong reputations they had built decades ago. However, with time, many HR agencies lost their purpose in favor of behavior which is difficult to assign to any organizational archetype. Many of them jeopardized trust and professional reputation for quick and easy deals and thus lost themselves.

Many HR agencies and consultants that claim to be experts in evaluating people are simply selling not knowledge and expertise but patterned inefficient processes that ultimately do not help clients. Clients do not trust the recruitment algorithms anymore. Low trust in their expertise has led the recruitment industry into a serious crisis. They do not fit into their archetypes and are not a good fit for any other typological form.

It began with a few HR agencies that succumbed to a number of bad habits at the beginning, damaging their relationship with their archetype. As a result, those few infected almost an entire industry.

What happened to Icebrit when it decided to go to the North Pacific? From a typology viewpoint, the problem is that Icebrit didn't sidestep the archetype, but it violated the assigned principle of location-dependent companies and tried jumping into an unfamiliar market where it had no experience or network. Location-dependent companies are tied up in particular locations and strive to be masters in their field. One can expand a location only after becoming familiar with a new geographical area; Icebrit bet everything on unexplored and unfamiliar ground.

Operational principle

Why are customers willing to pay a premium and remain loyal to one company and skeptical about a seemingly similar offer from another? Why do some people prefer shopping in big malls, another at boutiques and specialty shops, and another at discount stores?

How attractive an organization is depends on how well it fills its chosen niche. Does it understand what kind of company it is? What its operating principles are? What the needs of customers are. Do they know how to best utilize resources to accomplish their goals?

A customer is the main resource of any organization, in any industry, in any country. Customers define needs and pay organizations to satisfy them or solve their problems. A customer is a business's focal resource. Customer demand forms niches in the market for which the competition is fierce indeed.

How are organizations different in terms of operational principles and resource utilization? There are three types or clans of them - generalists, specialists, and scavengers.

Generalists enjoy market advantages satisfying average or more or less standard customers' requirements. In other words, generalists harvest low-hanging fruit as a result of their competitive position and don't feel the need to offer something extra to the market.

Bruce Lee, a famous American and Chinese actor, film director, martial artist, philosopher, and founder of the martial art Jeet Kune Do style once said, "I fear not the man who has practiced 10,000 kicks once, but I fear the man who has practiced one kick 10,000 times." In a business sense, we can say that generalists practice many kicks once, where specialists are masters of particular kicks trained over and over again.

Specialist companies work hard offering something novel and specific with some kind of additional value in order to satisfy customers. If you see a company always going the extra mile for customers, then most likely it will be a specialist. In other words, they offer hand-picked fruits.

Specialists exploit their niches to the fullest while contributing to the market, and are usually first with innovations, advanced solutions, and practices. For instance, technologies from racing cars are smoothly transferred to mass automotive production; their best practices become the norm for other companies across the industry; their mastery in customer engagement and satisfaction spread widely in time.

There are always some crumbs left over in any market. Scavenger companies are interested in extracting value from what is left over by more serious market players. They are not really embedded into a market and hence are not contributors to it, they're just in a constant search for discarded resources. Thus, they have few loyalties and their operational strategies are built on finding the lowest resource outlay.

The customers' flow and access to resources and a company's capability to utilize them in the most efficient manner define the success. The operational principle must be clearly defined and reflected in the structure, systems, imprinted capacities, and functions of a company.

In this sense, a specialist company like Icebrit made a mistake typical for many start-ups and even mature companies. Icebrit lost its understanding of the difference in operational principles needed in different businesses and locations. Its specialty in North Atlantic operations could not translate to the North Pacific.

Correct positioning defines how easily customers recognize an organization's product on the market, where a niche also reflects the relevant quality of a product or service and availability of resources in the market. In this sense, the central area of a market reflects the standardized consumers' taste and demands, where a periphery of resource space is defined by more specific requirements of consumers willing to get something unique.

A clear understanding of the organization's position allows a company to see changes in customer demand and react promptly. Resource space is not static and moves all the time with changes in technology, materials, and most of all, human demand. Thus, companies are always on the hunt for the most promising niches. For instance, in the case of GoPro, the company initially occupied an excellent niche with its cameras but failed to exploit and expand it effectively.

Size matters

Companies are grouped into families depending on their size. Size matters in terms of understanding an organization's capacities, potentials, and limits as well. Size reflects an ability to control a certain market share, i.e., an ability to serve a certain number of customers without loss of quality and efficiency. Thus, the size influences it goals and the scale of its tasks.

What a company can afford in terms of incorporating different management systems and fancy structures is also dictated by size. Differences in structure and processes will affect the formation of an organization. However, businesses don't always realize their limits and size-bounded restrictions, thinking of themselves as larger than they actually are; scaling up their operations without radical redesign and relevant change. This is a recipe for failure. For instance, medium-sized Icebrit stepped into the arena where the players were bigger, and the company fell after one hit from those heavyweight competitors.

However, most of the industry giants started small, even very small, such as Apple, Amazon, Microsoft, and many others. Besides being persistent they have one other thing in common – their initial framework allowed them to grow larger and adopt additional capacities. This was possible because their leaders envisioned the need for such changes from day one.

Not many can be as masterful, prepared, and heroic as David in his challenge against Goliath. Many dream about repeating the success of famous leaders, but not many are masterful in the fair evaluation of capacities, setting goals, achieving a sophisticated understanding of customers' needs and envisioning future trends, and preparedness for change.

Being savvy in customer relationships

Today, as never before, the importance of customer relations is at its peak. Every organization's employees must be customer relationships savvy, whether they interact directly with customers or not.

Whether a product is digital or comes from a factory, it is done by people, for people, and delivered through meaningful relationships. The system of external relationships forms the peripheral nervous system which is responsible for bringing the organization as close to customers as possible and allows for efficient resource acquisition.

An efficient peripheral system allows a company to treat customers with care. The excellence of the peripheral system reflects its capacity to maintain a productive relationship. The strength of the relationship defines the distance to external resources. The stronger the relationship, the closer the organization is to its customers.

The bigger the organization, the greater the number of external relations it has. However, all relations are different in their effect on the organization as they relate to their nature, characteristics, and strengths. There are three types of external relations - strong, intermediate, and weak.

Strong relations link a company with key customers and secure the flow of critical resources essential for adding value in the production process. They assist success through collaboration with key partners.

Strong ties are responsible for higher competitiveness and development prospects. These relations are very functional, emotionally intense, and have a great influence on reputation and positive recognition. We know that 20% of strong relations secure up to 80% of a business. At the same time, a number of strong relations for specialist companies can be greater, reaching 25%. The simplest way to evaluate the value of strong relations is to imagine the absence of them and the consequent impact on the company.

Most sales and profit-generating transactions are obtained through intermediate or value-adding relations. These ties are responsible for selling organizational products or services in larger volumes.

Intermediate relations are very functional and secure up to 40% of turnover or more depending on the archetype and industry nature. While these relations can be replaced without dramatic damage to the company's activity and profit, their role and importance shouldn't be underestimated and sacrificed for minute gain.

Growth is directly associated with the expansion of intermediate ties and the ability to exploit them. These relations are built on all invited parties understanding the product features and characteristics.

Random and irregular sales, external services, and suppliers that have no critical and direct impact on the organizational production process are considered as weak or service relations. Weak relations are the easiest to replace, while at the same time, they add a lot to expanding the customer base. They are important particularly for donor-dependent organizations for which every support is a great help, and location-dependent organizations surviving on small scale operations.

The healthy and efficient composition of all three types of relations in the company's portfolio allows it to stand firmly and grow in its market. If a company is losing strong relations and intermediate ones slip into weak, it is a clear sign that it needs to dramatically revise its approach to customer service.

The ability to maintain and develop organizational relationships comes with experience and age. It demands investments in employees' training, effort from the entire team, and most importantly - time. Durable relationships usually take at least a year to become evident and reach projected productivity. This is the minimum time needed to assess all the factors influencing the strength of the relationship and the aspects of mutual integrity, reciprocity, and profitability to become obvious for all parties involved – the company, customers, and partners.

Another difficult and time-consuming task during initial development is the need to devote time and effort to the continued maintenance and development of customer relations. Every relation must be analyzed in order to deliver tailor-made care since no one likes to be treated as a commodity.

Every transaction is a test allowing the company to prove its ability to fulfill its obligations towards customers in a professional manner and with the anticipated performance and quality levels. Such a test should be passed with a five-star rating.

Underperforming partners and suppliers whose poor performance may negatively affect the quality of customer service should be dropped before they undermine the whole business, instead of one or two transactions. Unreliable partners ruin your reputation, diminish your effort, and squander your investments. For instance, when a bank blames partners for a technical support failure then the customer questions the bank's ability to provide sufficient care for him and his money.

One of the reasons why start-ups and young companies are vulnerable is that they are dependent on the performance and operational excellence of their partners. Naturally, no partner is perfect, but those who consistently perform poorly are simply not acceptable.

What is the difference in maintaining customer relationships between specialist and generalist companies? In a majority of cases, the generalists are not greatly bothered about the development of strong relations with customers as the universe of potential resources is larger for them, and they are less concerned if a few of them must be replaced. At the same time, they can't afford juggling customers as their reputation is at stake. Companies that count on new customers to replace old ones forget that the demand for customer service is always high and unquestionably important become non-entities. For instance, US Airways, a once famous airline, decided to save on customer service which led to mistreated passengers and systematic ignorance of complaints. These issues drove its customers to the point where people didn't want to do business with the airline, driving it to bankruptcy in 2005.

The specialists maintain and develop stronger organizational relations with all partners where possible, especially with their customers and suppliers. They must squeeze everything out of the available resources and develop customer service expertise to survive in their niches. Their existence is defined by attention paid to customers.

When we talk about the importance of loyal customers, we shouldn't forget that the organization must be loyal to its customers as well as treating them individually. This is particularly important for specialists.

Scavengers are one-night stands. A scavenger's life cycle is short, making them opportunists looking for quick, short-term gain. Customers are aware of this and treat such companies the same way. There is not much positivity and support in their relations. Scavengers are playing the game of weak ties, having limited capacity for maintaining long-lasting, durable relations. They are not thinking about service quality or after-sales service. In their view, tomorrow is tomorrow, and we are living today only. These guys wouldn't worry if the customer feels cheated or not satisfied.

The business world is tough on those weak and incompetent in customer relations. If a company doesn't read customers or has difficulty understanding them, then the business has little chance to succeed. Thus, customer relationships must be revised very frequently, monthly or bi-monthly, for instance.

Central or internal nervous system

Effective governance with a human face relies on four internal processes – organizational cognition, control, internal communication, and organizational learning. These four elements form the central or internal nervous system and react to internal and external changes.

While acting simultaneously, these processes are responsible for reporting on the shortage of resources, changes in internal strength and capacity, risks, and consistency of performance. The central nervous system uses the information received from internal sensors (control systems) and external receptors (organizational relationships) to secure the desired efficiency and to enhance performance.

Organizational cognition is responsible for the direct interaction between knowledge developed within the organization and sensory processes. It coordinates organizational senses and judges conditions and problems using experience, rational processes, and professional expertise. Cognition defines how successfully a company adapts to market conditions and fulfills customers' needs using its existing capacities.

Control is the process of establishing and maintaining authority over the organization which requires the use of different assessments and analyzing systems to help managers make administrative decisions, sensing and signaling problems and show how effectively resources are gained and processed.

Internal communication is focused on the execution of tasks and processes, coordination of activities, and ensuring the employees support management decisions and actions taken. Internal communication secures the transmission of meanings across the company and timely and effective interaction between its members.

The ability to learn defines the organization's capability to settle organically into the environment and evolve with it. Learning is compulsory for survival. If an organization can't learn, then it becomes prey to more skillful competitors. Learning is an active and creative process that has two main concerns - the cost and value of knowledge, and the efficiency of knowledge transfer.

Conclusion

People develop by becoming more knowledgeable and by exercising their mind daily. Companies become successful by exploring their inner world and the environment around them. Business intelligence is in the ability to combine potentials with authentically imprinted strength and properties. Being authentic in nature and innovative in exploring potentials always pays off.

However, incompetent decision making can destroy any strong combination. Mistakes in treating and exploiting an archetype's properties, operational principles, size advantages, core processes, and external relations are harmful and will result in a dysfunctional organization.

Practical tips

- Don't look for the organization's limits, look for its potentials. The daily aim of every business is to explore the hidden internal and external potentials that allow development and new ways of satisfying customers.

- Capitalization reflects the quality of management decisions and actions directed for growth rather than chasing fancy trends and finding problems and limits.

- Always ask – Would our customers be happy and satisfied if we implement such and such decision? If you are doubtful, then customers' reactions will be doubtful or even negative.

- There is no such thing as distance relations with customers. The relations with remote customers must be meaningful and productive.

- What makes your customers believe in your company and remain loyal to them? Prove it daily through your actions. These would-be superstars who forget about their core and imprinted roles fall the hardest.

- Learn from industry leaders as they stay successful by being authentic and focused and thus, competitive.

- Customers are the fairest judges of the company's actions. If all is fine then their base is growing. If not, customers disappear without notice. Talk to them, ask for their help, and watch their reaction with full attention, particularly when exploring new territory.

Part Two

CORPORATE CULTURE

Have you ever searched for a key around the house while holding it in your hand? Almost certainly. This has happened to all of us, more than once.

I have seen the same situation in many companies that were looking for a means of performance improvement and growth while having everything they need in their hands. All they need was to turn to their culture. Culture is a master key that unlocks inner strength, performance, and growth potential, everything a company needs to attract and satisfy customers while improving day after day.

Strong culture unlocks every heart and every mind, stimulating employees and developing their competencies. In this sense, real leaders see cultivating culture as something requires attention every day. Yet it well worth any cost involved. Real leaders don't skimp on people, they nurture them through a strong culture.

Corporate culture serves people in a qualitative manner. If a company serves customers, it adds depth and warmth to the relationship. A strong culture makes customer relations more natural and meaningful. The more warmth and understanding corporate culture shares with customers, the more support it gets in return.

Culture is the soul and spirit of an organization and is the second element of the business trinity. It breathes life into relations and processes and thus, influences every aspect of the business.

Chapter Five

CORPORATE CULTURE: A MINISTRY OF HAPPINESS

Everyone sees corporate culture differently, like love or friendship. We look at this phenomenon from different angles while experiencing similar feelings of warmth, devotion, and commitment to others.

Often, even though we are affected by the strength and positivity of strong corporate culture we don't know how to articulate our feelings about it. It causes excitement and positive emotions we share with others. At the same time, positive culture is deeply personal and important for everyone and inspires us to care for it to the best of our abilities.

Corporate culture is about and for people. It isn't formal but is powerful enough to change horizons. Culture shapes people into one cohesive form which makes the company effective and more real to employee and customer alike. Without this critical element a company is just a legal form where disconnected people work for money.

Understanding of customers comes from human sensitivity and responsiveness to other's needs.

Customer's needs are not written somewhere and firmly declared. To understand customers and their demands, a company needs to actively engage them and consciously keep them at the center of its operations.

Soul and Spirit

I have heard the same peculiar statement many times – we don't have culture in our company. This is wrong. There is no such thing as an absence of culture in a company. Every company has culture. As soon as people begin interacting the culture is born. Whether it is positive or not, culture is always there.

What is culture? Culture is multidimensional and has many facets, where each one shines differently like a finely polished diamond. Again, culture is the soul and spirit of business. If we talk about business with a human face then culture is responsible for the humanity, personality, and charisma of the company.

Culture is the inner world of an organization and is unique for every business. At the same time, culture is an organization's energy, deriving from the effort, qualities, and competencies of all employees combined and channelled to achieve the company's goals.

Culture connects people's hearts and minds in their actions. It serves as a catalyzer of performance making human relations meaningful, productive, and rich in positive emotions whether among colleagues or in relations with customers. It breathes life into formal processes, hierarchical dependencies, and daily routines. Positive culture serves as a ministry of happiness for employees and customers as well.

Culture offers an incredibly high return on investment – ROC (Return on Culture). The more we put into it the more we get from it. Every effort and input counts. In terms of performance and efficiency, we already learned that cost-cutting in a race for efficiency can kill a business, particularly small ones. Culture secures effectiveness through engaged collaboration beyond the boundaries of formal job execution. Simultaneously, it teaches people how to be useful for others, supporting and guiding the company through turbulent times.

By engaging people culture fosters such indispensable resources as trust, professionalism, teamwork, shared vision, accountability, innovativeness, and preparedness for change.

The power posture of a strong company is based on employees' pride in their organization. If they work for a wealthy but not people-focused company, it gives them status and pay but without a sense of fulfilment. If the company stands strong because of its culture, people will be confident that together they will overcome any challenges that may come.

Why important

One of the most serious mistakes from the past is neglecting the role of culture. Sadly, the promise of money comes first for most businessmen and culture is far from the top of the list. However, neglecting culture actually negatively affects the money that can be made.

Successful strategy is based on emphasising human involvement in every process, operation, or transaction. Competitive advantages derive from people and their competencies and not in processes.

If one doesn't understand the paramount role of culture in business, the people will be neglected. Ignoring culture means disconnecting the trinity of business from itself and from customers.

Who builds the culture?

Initially, culture is envisioned and initiated by a leader. This is only the beginning of this long journey where a head office picks up the responsibility over strengthening corporate culture.

A corporate head office is often called a Power House. Its duty is to get all the power of an organization together and direct it in accordance with the company's goals. It defines how effective people should work together to achieve the company's goals. Leaders are rewarded for developing that incredible corporate power through people and their input into their development.

Today's leaders' motto sounds simple – "I am going to be the best for employees and customers. I care for people on their terms, not mine."

Leaders are role models in maintaining culture. Before declaring that the company has a strong culture, a leader should model how to take care of it, show personal involvement, share experience, and embrace culture together with people.

Leaders lay cornerstones and pillars of culture and employees lay the bricks through engagement and involvement. Encouraging cultural development demands involvement and input from every person in the company.

Employees are transmitters of the leader's understanding and vision of culture. Employees amplify the leader's cultural message – if it is strong, they will make it stronger, if negative then it will be more negative.

Employees are not spectators or irrelevant users of culture. Everyone in the company is an ambassador. Every employee should champion the culture, encouraging others in the way they work. Every corporate citizen should feel responsible for the creation of that culture and enjoy its fruits. Engagement in cultural cultivation must be clearly articulated and rewarded appropriately. Unfortunately, this is often forgotten.

It is essential that everyone understands culture as a shared responsibility. Culture must be maintained and cultivated by all company members. Employees are happier and more fulfilled when they genuinely feel like part of a team rather than a collection of isolated individuals.

I was talking to Nancy, the branch manager of one of the British banks. Nice lady, clever, and enthusiastic. She consistently repeated "I" and never said "we" discussing the branch's life.

I asked – "Why do you never say 'us' talking about your team?"

She became a little bit confused and said, "… This is purely my fault from the past. I should confess that I am a finance person and not an expert in managing people. Plus, our bank is like a fast-food shop where people come and go often. My colleagues are well aware of the situation.

"Just a year ago when I stepped into the role, I had a little chance to pull a team together and used only my human senses for this. It worked to some extent but not as well as I hoped. I took the online course in people management. The improvements are there, and I feel my colleagues' enthusiastic support. You are right. I learned very well that culture and environment in the branch is my responsibility and it is great to be supported by the team. Today, we are the team of us, and I am proud of my colleagues and myself."

Business and customers are co-creators of culture

Business is a social creature, where corporate culture is responsible for defining the rules of engagement and interaction between employees and with customers. Business thrives off interaction and lives because of it. For instance, try to book a room by calling a hotel directly and in most cases, you will have a similar or even better deal than those offered by different hospitality or bookings platforms. Hotels value you taking the time to engage them directly and are eager to engage in turn.

Employees and customers are creators and consumers of culture. Customers are those deserving and expecting to be served with positivity and understanding of their needs, where employees are internal customers and shareholders of culture with a profound interest in its growth.

Culture leverages employees' competencies and abilities with customers' expectations. In this sense, employees and customers are co-creators of culture. Customers guide culture through their comments and suggestions while employees react by attempting to respond positively.

Customers are the inspirers of culture, motivators of cultural change, and the source of any reward for performance. A company and its employees are architects and constructors of that culture.

Customers' business dealings are based on expectations of being served by those who understand their demands.

It is nonsense that employees should have difficulty understanding customers. Every individual is an employee and customer at the same time, just in different circumstances. After office hours, employees become customers while they shop, travel on a train, visit a bank, or visit a medical consultant. I am still puzzled why many managers have difficulty understanding customers and don't reflect on their own experience.

For instance, we all use banks. Certainly you have faced a situation where a bank manager talked to you using terminology you don't understand while finding excuses not to address your simple request. I've faced this situation many times. I wonder how these people talk at home with family. Probably, something like this – "due to the unforeseen technical problems, caused by a retail supplier of our family and delays in service, our daily inventory of milk and bread can't be renewed. You, my family, should understand the problem and wait until it is resolved."

Sounds funny but this happens all the time in business. Simply, never leave your humanity at home. Win hearts by meeting customers with a responsive customer-focused culture.

Cultural Values

Think for a moment that when we get married, we accept family values such as love, mutual support, and respect to build a future for our spouses and children. Happy spouses motivate and encourage each other. Initially, we learn about family values from parents and discuss them with future partners well before saying "I do." If there are no such values in a marriage, it quickly turns sour and falls apart, and no force can hold it together.

What happens when one gets into a new job and wants to know about the culture? When accepting a job offer, we should aim to know as much as possible about the inner life of the company. What values does the culture stand for? Values show the aspirations of the culture and help bring employees together.

Cultural values reflect how people see relationships and their personal role in them, whether in the context of organizational or social life (see also Corporate Superpower, 2018). The aim of cultural values is to stimulate employees and encourage a willingness to commit their capabilities to the achievement of the organization's goals and serving others.

Values are the stars the company uses to navigate the rough seas of business and everyday challenges without losing itself. These stars point the way to the future the company is striving for. Today's values define tomorrow's reality and unite future generations in its creation.

Values make every employee feel part of something important, encouraging them to proudly share them with customers. They define and guide hierarchical, peer-to-peer, customer, and stakeholder relationships.

Values are the best and most consistent predictors of human desires and needs. While stepping into the V2V (values-to-values) era, businesses aim to match their values with their customers as close as possible. Otherwise, if company values are not in line with the customers' expectations, then the distance between the business and its customers will remain unsurmountable.

While articulating corporate values it is important to run some kind of feasibility test, asking to whom values are addressed, why and how they appeal to people, why they are important for employees and customers, and their importance today and in the years ahead. Values are addressed by people to people and are not merely for individual use. They must be very appealing and deeply touch human feelings. How values are understood and accepted by both groups of people, employees and customers, define their viability and relevance to the business. At their best, values connect generations and thus, must be timeless at their basic level.

Value-efficiency or time-efficiency

This section may sound a bit philosophical, but businesses need to reach a new understanding of the roles of values to reach the desired levels of customer service.

Values stand outside time. Values, not time, define our obligations towards colleagues and customers. Real values are transcendent, encouraging people to act for things beyond themselves.

If we use time as a reference point, then we are bound by it whether something is done with high quality or not. If we take values as the reference, then we think of completing a task or reaching a goal only when it is done up to a certain standard and customers are fully satisfied.

Measuring effort in customer service against a clock is one thing, where measuring the same service against the fulfillment of values opens a completely new dimension in developing customer relations and level of care. How would you evaluate a deeply meaningful conversation with a person you highly admire - in quality of thoughts explored and discussed or in time spent with this person? Most likely you will remember the quality of the conversation. In this sense, values represent what most satisfies us, and are worth even more than time.

Quality of customer service, even a single experience, is qualified by satisfaction, and overall positivity. Time spent caring for customers to fulfill values is never wasted and is always rewarding.

One is prepared for doing much more with greater effort and without question while following values, whereas time constrains effort and limits commitment. A customer-centered approach and people-centered leadership are focused on values and not on time. Focusing on time as the main value negatively affects the quality of human interactions and diminishes the role of values. Time constraints don't make people happy.

Foreseeing changes in the role of culture

What will the future bring us? The most obvious answer is – change. It may be turbulent or steady but certainly change. I don't know any human generation that hasn't lived in a time of change. It is an inevitable part of human life.

Corporate culture is not an exception. Culture changes along with growing demand. As we are heading towards an increasingly digital marketplace, we must consider factors that influence the need for change, at least those foreseeable in the near future.

- Modern business demands breakthrough performance where the main potentials are found in a productive culture.

- The existing level of performance is not sufficient and advanced human qualities and competencies must be mobilized to compete.

- Competitive advantages praised yesterday are not unique anymore. Unique advantages are in people and the ability to engage them.

- Increased demand for sophisticated customer service has only begun. Corporate culture needs to require every employee to make such service a personal responsibility.

- A workplace is no longer merely a desk with computer and phone. The future workplace will have additional options of direct collaboration with colleagues, customers, even those remotely located. Employee competencies will be developed, and innovation encouraged in order to improve customer service.

- Changes in understanding of culture will generate demand for rethinking its changing nature and functions.

However, the World Economic Forum report (18 September 2018) shows that "While enormous resources are being spent on digital transformation programs by the private sector, the results are underwhelming. According to estimates, this year over $1.2 trillion will be spent by companies worldwide on their digital transformation efforts and yet analysis suggests that only 1% of these efforts will actually achieve or exceed their expectations."

According to this insightful study, businesses still confuse their product with customer needs, that need determines the value of the product, not the product the need. This in turn drives a corporate need to innovate, not only in the products themselves but in how the company interacts with customers. All these needs are drivers of corporate culture and new methods of exploring its potentials are urgently needed.

Practical tips

- Business is a system of relationships for the future. Business as a cold transaction is not sufficient anymore.

- Change the company from the inside out if demanded by the need to satisfy customers and thus make it a new being every day, at every stage of development.

- Cultural competencies are always demanded and highly praised at any business. One can take professional skills and competencies to another job but the ability to grasp and develop cultural competencies is more important and more difficult to gain.

- Values will not help if they must be imposed from above. Values must reach hearts and minds, not just pocketbooks.

- Persistence in following values pays now and pays even greater in the long run. Uniting employees in one strong force and getting closer to customers depends on values. Every little step towards them can be capitalized handsomely.

Chapter Six

CARE AND ENGAGEMENT: A CURRENCY OF CULTURE

For years, I was absolutely confident that we prefer to stay quiet about the existence of negative culture in many businesses, or what I call the Dark Kingdom, which destroys companies one after another every day. However, I was wrong. The modern demand for cultivating strong culture showed a harsh side effect where the artificial or superficial forms of culture emerged.

Not long ago I was asked by a newly appointed CEO to help with restoring strong culture and bringing the business back from brink of disaster.

The previous CEO was very eager to decorate his CV with expertise in the development of culture. He was thinking about some kind of a show for the board of directors, and nice records for a potential employer rather than actual effort in cultivating strong culture. The ex-CEO received an excellent seven-figure "good-bye" package while his work was nicely evaluated based on the reports of his three supporters, Marketing Director, HR Director, and Business Development Director. No one bothered to talk with line managers and workers.

Reality proved to be different than reported as this CEO was far better at pretending to care about culture that about culture itself. He actually managed to break the main pillars of culture – people engagement, commitment, and simple positivity. The artificial culture of double standards and made-up reports was fake and suicidal for the company.

I talked to almost one hundred employees of this company to learn their views and concerns. The result was shocking. The vast majority of people with whom I have talked considered corporate culture after their last experience a big lie to make people the slaves of the company. Some of the respondents even mentioned they felt like guinea pigs for management.

To make a long story short, despite such a tough ordeal the culture picked up and showed the signs of flourishing. Working with this case I learned a great lesson. Not every workplace has a positive culture, and no one should be tagged as an unworthy person just because he or she has worked in a toxic place that no one with strong self-esteem would tolerate. However, no company, no leader should be allowed to kill people's hope in something positive and leave the scorched souls behind.

Thinking about this case from different angles I realized how important care is for people. They need it. As soon as care is missing in company-employee relations people close their souls and minds, becoming entirely defensive.

Care

Care is a commodity a company offers its employees over and above a wage. People judge the company based on how it cares for them. Employees will engage only if the company is fully engaged in them. If no care exists in relation to employees, then no engagement can be expected in return.

While this sounds simple, care is one of the most puzzling issues for leaders in terms of how to understand and express it in the most efficient and appealing way.

Care is action, not words only. Care is a verb expressing actions for others. Let's focus on five core aspects of care critically important for cultivating positive corporate culture – involvement in people, concern for their future, emotional comfort, physical comfort, and safety.

- The real nature of the company is seen in its ability to care for people, not in words. Acting effectively for people means knowing what people need and supporting them in their desires. Being close to people should be a leadership priority. Leaders should regard it a privilege to get know their employees, to listen, reflect, and act for them.

Involvement begins with engaging interaction. A few minutes of genuine interaction are worth years of formal communication. Make every minute worth a year.

This is similar to a friendship in which strong understanding of each other comes into play. Being connected and involved means partnering with employees on a full range of issues that have an impact on human life. This kind of care can affect personal and professional growth.

Caring about people and their lives and career prospects can't be faked. No one would believe in a "Santa Claus-style" leader who they see once a year, especially one likely to be bearing bad news.

Building rapport and understanding demands daily involvement. To feel and understand people one should always have a place for them in his own mind and heart. Inconsistency in involvement undermines the consistency and efficiency of relations.

- Thinking of people's future is a must for every organization. A company with positive culture aims to increase the value of its people every day. This is absolutely necessary for making a company attractive to current and future employees.

A company is not a shop that buys and sells people's commitment. If people think of their loyalty as being a matter of price, they will only perform to the level they think their pay is worth. The company is a place where people grow by finding the best use of their talents. The company is a nursery where talents, competencies, and qualities are cared for by capable leaders.

Care is personal. Every individual has his or her own potentials, desires, actual limits for change and improvement, and vision for the future. Therefore, a general approach to people will not work as well as it might have in the past. Care assumes acting while clearly understanding every person as an individual.

The logic is straightforward. All of us offer our personal competencies to an employer expecting support in professional and personal growth. Every person tends to ask – How do I benefit from working for a given company? How does it help me now, and in the future?

This demands taking people as they are while clearly focusing on their strengths and finding joy in giving people what they need for growth and thus not over or undervaluing employees' qualities and competencies.

- Emotional comfort. Full care cannot be imagined without caring about the inner state of employees, their psychological and mental comfort. Their emotional comfort is determined by the openness of the organization's inner climate, positivity of emotions, respect, consistency of leadership, and ease of interaction at all hierarchical levels.

If you want people to smile today, then be positive yesterday. Let employees leave the office smiling, and they will smile as they come in the next day. Caring for employees' emotional comfort celebrates people and the inner richness they bring to the company. Care of emotional comfort means multiplying inner human capacity and aspiration for performance.

Keeping employees under stress, sucking all their inner energy by shouting and swearing at them, can lead them into depression and kill engagement.

Ruining positive emotions and insulting employees is far too common in many modern offices. Unfortunately, too many so-called leaders use this approach and are surprised by low levels of employee engagement. They forget that no salary can cover a loss of dignity and confidence and that they lose people as a result.

- Physical comfort of people was a top priority of my superintendent, Jim Newcomb, from my old days at sea. He used to say that people are not mushrooms to be kept in the dark and fed with shit. Jim was very concerned about the state of the cabins, food, uniform, tools, and much more. He was right, and I still recall the way he cared for his crew's physical comfort and how we repaid him with full commitment to the job.

Physical comfort is important for anyone. Enough light, minimal distractions, feeling comfortable, chance to relax during breaks, appropriate location, or other factors allow people to feel and perform well.

Certainly, some limitations can be acceptable such as in a start-up with a limited budget. However, this is not acceptable for a mature company. No one will be productive and inclined to work in an uncomfortable environment of packed and noisy offices. The first thing that comes into the minds of employees is that the company saves money on them for a fatter profit.

- Safety is an element of active care that reflects professionalism in people management. Safety, it may sound very formal, even bureaucratic. However, if you don't see safety as a valuable part of care then talk to people and imagine how you would look in the eyes of a wife who lost her husband because of the company's carelessness. Safety has an incredibly broad impact. Besides the direct importance for employees, safety is important to families, relatives, and society.

Safety reflects lessons from the past and the wisdom of previous generations in terms of the employees' confidence in a secure environment. High attention to safety shows that no one would risk the employees' life, health, and well-being for the sake of a quick gain. Also, as one of my friends, a CFO of a large energy corporation said to me – "A company which scores best on safety also scores best on performance." It is relevant to every industry and not only to those high-risk professions such as soldiers, fishermen, pilots, etc.

The level of care determines the functionality of corporate culture. Positive culture shows its functionality through the real care of people. Negative or artificial cultures never care for anyone except bosses. People see their leaders engaged and caring for them and engage in return. If leaders turn their backs to people who constantly need their help and support, then no productive collaboration and mutual engagement can be expected.

The higher the degree of care then the higher the level of employees' engagement will be. It answers the question of why organizations with negative culture are low in long-term performance. Disengaged people never perform at their best.

I talked to more than one hundred people from different countries, industries, and ranks aiming to find how care is important and how it is implemented. The most common approach people take is benchmarking their best experience to their present conditions. If the situation is regarded as worse, people become cross and suspicious, questioning even promising changes. They sense a threat in everything and withhold engagement for better times.

Care of employees is a sign of strong relations between a company and its employees. It gives people a sense of being part of a team while regarding everyone as a unique and valuable member of that team at the same time. One feels cared for when one knows that someone is thinking of him and shares in his feelings, affections, and worries.

Engagement

Engagement is a currency that employees pay back to a company that genuinely cares. The higher the engagement of employees, the higher the business's value as its workforce becomes more valuable and effective.

Someone may say that we are repeating the same things again and again. However, we tend to forget that any currency tends to lose its value with time. The value of engagement also tends to depreciate with time if we don't reinforce and infuse it with new meaning. Exploring new meanings of engagement gives it more strength and empowers the workforce to produce excellent work for themselves, the company, and customers.

What happens in reality? While working with different companies, I found that a patterned understanding of engagement doesn't work as effectively as expected. We repeat the same mantras about engagement, and it becomes less appealing to people and sounds more like preaching from pushy managers. Whatever impressed people once gets dated with time and demands new impressions and meanings to jumpstart employees' potentials. If we want to grow in our own and customers' eyes, then we must rethink how we consider engagement.

Exploring new meanings of engagement and its components is the duty of every leader, not once in a while but as a constant. This is necessary to keep people inspired and motivated. A new enriched understanding of engagement and its components allows acceleration of employees' development and growth. The resulting personal development is genuinely rewarding.

No one can win the battle for customers using dated rules and principles. Customer demands constantly change, and the only thing that remains permanent is the demand for more sophisticated collaboration between business and its customers. Thus, enriched understanding of engagement drives the company to new heights in customer excellence.

People change and their demands change as well. I love the George Bernard Shaw (*Man and Superman*, 2018) quote – "The only man I know who behaves sensibly is my tailor; he takes my measurements anew each time he sees me. The rest go on with their old measurements and expect me to fit them." Don't offer people the same system of evaluating and encouraging them without understanding how they have changed. See how they have grown and offer something new.

Let's look at how such components of engagement as job satisfaction, loyalty, creativity, responsibility, shared affection and support, and preparedness to change can be viewed differently. It may look simple but finding new meanings is never easy, but is always rewarding.

Job satisfaction

Job satisfaction can be measured against the simple question - how strongly I want to be at my workplace tomorrow regardless of today's problems. What I feel at the end of the day and how proud I am of what I do makes a whole lot of difference.

Practically everyone who is satisfied sees their as work meaningful and productive. According to the Petri Böckerman and Pekka Ilmakunnas (2012) research on the satisfaction-to-productivity ratios highly meaningful work annually generates an additional $9,078 per worker.

There is no job satisfaction without positivity. More positivity leads to greater and more consistent success. People want to feel that their work attracts attention and earns the gratitude of their bosses and customers. What can be more satisfying than seeing satisfied customers and feeling like you are making a difference in people's lives?

It is important for everyone to become visible and recognized for what they do, to feel they are needed. On the other hand, the collaborative effort to solve problems only increases individual willingness to work for the company.

At the end of the day, people are satisfied if they love what they are doing and see it having a positive effect on the lives of others.

Creativity

Ideas that change the world come from bold and brave thinkers. Those creatives who think outside the box disrupt the world with their solutions to problems. Their imaginations never sleep, offering solutions in engineering, operations, people management, sales, marketing, and many other fields.

Creativity means finding new forms of expressing love and care to customers to allow greater understanding of the customer's feelings and unspoken desires.

I was watching a YouTube video on education. According to it, kids hear "no" 150,000 times and they only hear "yes" 5,000 times before reaching their seventeenth birthday. Can you imagine how this might restrict human creativity?

It led me to wonder if anything changes when we enter the workforce. Actually, not much does change, particularly in companies with negative culture. The culture that kills creativity has many "no's" and only a few "yes's" like – "can I work longer hours without pay?"– "yes"; "can I forget about a bonus"– "yes"; "am I responsible for every problem" – "yes." In terms of hearing "no" – "can I get trained to be promoted?" – "no, we have other plans"; "do you value my work?" – "no, you are not better than others"; "may I offer some innovative idea?" – "no, we work on certain standards and prescribed procedures."

Thus, negative culture is the culture of thousands of "no's" where positive culture aims to respond with "yes" to new ideas. The company that doesn't welcome creativity becomes blind and helpless in terms of development.

Creativity is a gifted way of thinking and working outside the routine. These people need help to pull them up rather than be pushed down with bureaucracy and rigid formalization. They need help to reveal and exploit their potential and foster innovativeness.

Think for a moment, how would you deal with the next brave idea coming from an employee or colleague that may change the status quo and better serve your customers?

Responsibility

In September 2018, a drop in cabin pressure was noticed on the International Space Station (ISS) with six astronauts on board. The problem was caused by a small hole in the hull of the Russian-built Soyuz MS-09 spacecraft, in the Russian section of ISS. The crew rushed to fill the hole with a special type of epoxy.

The crew was initially blamed for making the hole, but later it was proved that drilling the hole in zero gravity is impossible. Then the problem was admitted being a production error though the culprits weren't identified. The hole was masked with a sealant which had fallen off after the craft docked with the ISS. It wasn't a simple technical fault but almost a fatal irresponsibility that put six people's lives and a tremendously expensive expedition in jeopardy.

An old formula, more responsibility means twice the work, is still valid. The only change in this formula is that responsibility for one's own actions or lack thereof has transformed into the responsibility-360 mode. Responsibility-360 means being responsible towards the company, colleagues, customers, and potential impact beyond the direct effect - it means all-around responsibility.

Responsibility is expected as customers trust businesses to meet their needs. Thus, every employee should be held responsible to the extent he or she helped to solve the customer problem, how the quality of work reflects the understanding of the company's goals and mission, and how positively she impacts customer relations.

Those empowered and nurtured by positive culture are the most responsible for it. If a strong culture and the support of colleagues helped you to grow, then your responsibility is to help others as well. Strong culture assumes everyone is willing to help others.

Slackness at work is possibly or even more harmful than a genuine mistake. Both can lead to production bottlenecks and a decline in performance. Today, if every single employee is not adding value to the final product then talking about overall company effectiveness is meaningless. This is a danger even in positive cultures and often the first sign of a developing negative culture.

All of us are responsible for the future we create. Think for a moment that the hole in the ISS was drilled long before it was discovered. Imagine if in twenty years you're fixing mistakes someone made today. Doing good work today means saving yourself and others headaches in the future.

Preparedness for change

The speed of environmental, social, and technological changes is incredible, and we face a necessity for rapid change much more than any other generation before. On one hand, change is a response to life's inevitable challenges. On the other hand, change is discovery itself. This is a discovery of our own potentials, exploring new, exciting opportunities, and getting stronger every time.

Despite general acceptance that we all need change, not everyone is up to it at a personal level. This drags the modern business down like a weight tied to one leg. However, we continue to praise those who embrace change.

Those not prepared for change resist it if they are content with the current state of affairs. *What is in it for me personally? Why should I change for myself and for others, in particular?* They think of change as like jumping into ice-cold water.

In general, all people realize the need for change but often hesitate to ask for help. Willingness to change and the ability to do so are not always the same. Because of this, any change should be carefully managed.

Offer clearly articulated help to those facing doubts. A bright picture of a prospective future is not enough for these people. They need the help of those who have who have seen similar changes before. They need help understanding the need for change, in making the first steps, and help in the evaluation of achievements. Proper management greatly enhances the ability to accept change.

Someone who is changing has an influence and impact on many. The one who is not changing is only increasing the price of resentment for things that were not done. Those feeling safe in their comfort zone should remember that it soon becomes a rat's den full of dogmas and biases against development that will hamper personal and professional growth.

Loyalty

Loyalty is a hard-won relationship between company and employee. Loyalty is a gift that can be easily lost if taken-for-granted. Earning it is a daily and never-ending task.

Loyal employees are empathetic to their company and put a great deal of effort into it. Loyal people walk in the company's shoes and actively work for its goals without ignoring its problems.

There is no actual engagement without loyalty. Today, the center of gravity has shifted from employer to employee. The understanding of loyalty has also evolved, reflecting the authenticity of caring relations and advanced form of reciprocity in the company-employee relationship.

While pay is still critically important, the level of care offered by the company to the employee is becoming more significant. Being loyal means taking care of the company. At the same time, the company should pay for the employee's loyalty with the same coin assuming wider responsibility towards people. In other words, the company must be loyal to its employees as well.

What does it mean to be loyal to employees?

Firstly, this is a kind of chemistry between employee and company. Employees need to have not one, not two, but many reasons to become and remain loyal. They need exceptionally valid reasons to fully invest their knowledge, competencies, ideas, and effort into the company.

Secondly, loyalty implies the employee's belief in the company's future, and his future with it.

Thirdly, it should be a non-defensive dialogue between company and employee. If an employee accepts a company's problems, then it should tolerate non-critical employee mistakes and aid in correcting them. The non-defensive form of interaction cultivates mutual understanding and attachment. This shows respect and allows both company and employee to grow.

Fourthly, there is no loyalty without mutual respect for company and employee. Everyone plays his own role in this world and this deserves respect. Reminding people of your power over them only displays arrogance and kills loyalty.

Shared affection and support

Shared affection and support is the essence of engagement. Being valued and supported provides a sense of purpose and increases effort. No one can grow personally or professionally being alone. While aiming to grow, we need the support of colleagues and friends, support beyond simple things like taking a call, passing a file or an occasional pat on a shoulder.

Think of self-confidence. A confident person is a no-limit person, who builds competencies and achievement on top of achievement. Such a person knows well his capacity and potentials. We all need the support of others and their help to realize who we are and our own capabilities and potentials. We need the help of others to realize our own strengths and weaknesses, blind spots which we don't see. We simply need encouraging words when facing challenging situations, praise for achievements, and a fair evaluation of our ideas.

Colleagues are stakeholders of each other's success and contributors of each other's growth. By helping others, we grow stronger ourselves. Shared affection means that colleagues believe in us and their support goes far beyond purely personal interest. A team's support revitalizes existing strengths and reveals potentials.

We can't close the skills gap without strong workplace support and people being passionate about helping colleagues to grow. Many sources claim that 70% of employees get on-the-job training and professional knowledge from colleagues and peers. This is particularly important for the development of specific skills and competencies.

How much of yourself are you prepared to invest in others? What difference have you made for others? These are key questions for evaluating support in the modern workplace. Shared affection and support reflect how positively we influence and serve each other at work.

Conclusion

Care is an act of generosity initiated by a company with the goal of engaging people. Care is a form of pay-it-forward relations between the company and its employees which spreads to its customers, employees' families, competitors, and far beyond industry boundaries.

The aim of care is to engage people, involving everyone in generating value for customers. Care sets the standards of positive thinking and acting inside and outside of the organization. Formal care is only a meaningless decoration that fails to inspire.

Engagement is a voluntary response to the care of responsible corporate citizens. This invaluable response must be clearly appreciated to encourage those engaged and motivate those disengaged for involvement in win-win company-employee relations.

Both care and engagement are acts of giving with three beneficiaries – company, employees, and customers.

Practical tips

- New meanings given to care and engagement help to make firm steps in the development of people and as well as organizations. Think of them every time you plan any change.

- The leader's positive attention toward people and care of them are the vehicles of culture. When the leader is really passionate about people, employees, and customers, then maintaining and cultivating strong and engaging culture becomes a natural choice.

- Engaged employees become the customers' co-workers building customer satisfaction.

- Loyal employees create customer loyalty. They transform care received from the company into the even more valuable care of customers. Thus, loyalty has a wide-spread effect.

- Power posturing towards employees causes resistance rather than engagement. In this sense, when leaders care more about their own status than for people it costs a company millions.

- Simulated care causes simulated engagement. No one will pay high-value currency for cheating. This is the tit-for-tat nature of company-employee relations.

- The difference between employees and company behavior is that employees can simulate genuine engagement. This is a false engagement that will only be revealed by the company's decreasing profit margins.

Chapter Seven

DIFFERENT FACES OF CULTURE

*"Sometimes, we are so attached to our way of
life that we turn down wonderful opportunities
simply because we don't know what to do with it."*
—Paulo Coelho

Wining a close game isn't done by staying in your comfort zone. Your competitors already know all your usual tactics. A strong team will be able to use its strengths in a unique and unforeseen way. A unique culture makes a unique team that will always outperform competitors.

Productive corporate culture should be people-centered, flourishing, and living. A one-size fits all approach, trying to match the culture to something read in a book is a boring and lifeless substitute.

Only such a culture is truly alive and capable of lifting up people, allowing them to achieve ever greater things. It is alive and characterised with a great attitude and enormous potentials. If culture is not living and applied properly, it gradually becomes toxic, poisoning all within reach and destroying a business in the blink of an eye.

During the consultancy goal setting sessions with my clients I often hear a request – "we want the culture company X has. They are doing great and we want the same." My response is always the same – never try to fit into a mold if you want to succeed. Recognize that your business is unique and as such needs a unique culture. Your company is destined for a specific role for customers and thus many factors must be considered to enhance the effectiveness of culture.

The thing is that while cultivating a strong culture, a company needs to consider its purpose and what strengths should be elaborated taking into consideration the difference in organizational types, operational strategies, as well as the peculiarities of the local context. Without considering these factors the ultimate power of culture can't be realized. Copying and pasting culture is a waste of time and effort that creates more problems than it solves. Let's look at these differences to avoid culture mismanagement.

Culture's nuances of different types of businesses

The deeper you dive into the world of corporate culture, the more fascinating and interesting things you will see. This is like diving into unfamiliar waters. Saying that one corporate culture has the same mode and patterns as another is absolutely wrong. It has millions of faces and nuances, where specific archetypes reflecting the differences in the nature of a given business, how a product is developed and delivered, and how customer demand is understood and fulfilled and the unique development behind it.

Let's take a short tour across six different types of organizations – supermarkets, estate development and construction, food producers, tech producers, universities, and charities to look at the nuances of their cultures taking it as a general guideline of how culture differs from one type of business to another, and how it reveals the personality of each business.

Supermarkets

Customers always want to pay less and enjoy more. Whether people go shopping, or travelling for business or holiday across continents, or are at home on the internet, they want convenience and a positive experience. Modern sophisticated and educated customers consider every little detail. These customers demand that all location-dependent organizations must be always on their toes, always improving. Every penny is counted, and costs are strictly monitored.

Let's imagine what type of pressure a store's staff faces when serving thousands of shoppers in a busy day or the stress of a popular resort hotel staff when a few hundred tourists are partying day after day. Beside these psychological factors, retail offers very slim chances for career progression. People quickly get tired and leave such jobs as soon as possible.

This type of job represents a very young demographic due to the low entry requirements and permanent high demand for low-paid jobs. Inexperienced new employees coming in daily without sufficient training and life experience causes problems with customer service. Conflicts with customers are common, and they are insufficiently prepared to solve them. A positive corporate culture is even more important in these kinds of high turnover situations.

At the same time, a growing demand for the best customer solutions in line with the desires of local customers remains high as a matter of survival in this very competitive industry. Innovation becomes synonymous with exceeding expectations. It is not easy, but it is possible. For instance, Jack Ma was told many times that Chinese people would not use online shopping. In response he developed Alibaba, one of the most valuable corporations in the world.

In any context, customers demand genuine care on the part of any company they interact with. This is a voice that should come from the very inside of the organization and reflect a strong culture of care for people in it. In this sense, there are two cores that should be strongly considered when cultivating productive culture in a retail organization – focus on customers and cost saving - which demand effective solutions for customers and employees as well.

Employees, particularly short-term, think very little about reducing costs. Unfortunately, they don't think of how that raises costs for customers but focus instead on making their own lives comfortable. It would be more productive to build a culture that focuses on improving the customer experience overall. This is easier for even temporary workers to relate to as they are also customers.

Solutions and convenience should be created to serve people. Employees are internal customers of a retail organization. All potential solutions should be tested on them first and then offered to shoppers. Modern retail demands more prominent and effective solutions for training and enhancing staff in different areas such as precise timing, process optimization, and effective communication with customers.

These actions will improve staff turnover as people will feel involved in something more important than shifting boxes across shelves, and it will create a customer focused environment.

Food producers

Most of us are strongly tied to our tastes, whether it is bread, meat, fruits, sausages, soft drinks, cookies, or any other food. There is not much innovation in traditional production concerning taste and only very small changes in recipes can be seen over a long period of time. The recipes remain the same for decades. Coca-Cola, Yorkshire pudding, Campbell soup, Budweiser beer, or New York apple pie are much the same as our grandparents used to experience.

Traditional food producers are in a race to improve presentation and save costs as their product price and profit were predefined years ago. Thus, mainly changes in packing can be seen more and more often, and the dynamics of the food industry are dependent on how companies address cost saving culture.

Process effectiveness is critical, authenticity is vitally important, and excellence in quality is a must for food producers. All costs are weighed and justified, every cent is counted, and the bigger the operation the more important these issues are.

What type of corporate culture is appropriate for a food producer? There are four aspects of corporate culture that distinguish traditional food producers – preserving authenticity, mentoring, excellence in quality, and lean production.

First imagine the customer, where a product's authenticity in terms of taste, recipe, and experience come as a priority. Therefore, to survive and succeed, a food producer should think of one of its core cultural values as preservation of authenticity from generation to generation. Preservation of authentic taste is a matter of survival. I don't know any company that ignored traditional customers' tastes and experimented with anything new and succeeded.

If authenticity is passed from generation to generation, it develops a reputation for quality workmanship. This is a type of business where a lot of knowledge and competencies cannot be developed by learning from books, and mainly comes with experience. Mentoring is critically important in such an environment. Mentors pass on their skills to their apprentices over a long time. A food producer will fail without this strongly cultivated culture of high-level craftsmanship.

A consistently high level of craftsmanship is naturally praised by employees and customers alike. The employees can be proud of their work, and the customers are satisfied that they spent their time and money well.

Every stage of production must be perfect and efficient. Producers must be very innovative in cost-saving while securing overall efficiency of production. Yet, efficiency must never be sought at the expense of quality.

Tech producers

Tech companies represent a concentration of bright and highly talented professionals; those who are accustomed to solving complex problems and looking to the future with every action they take in the present. This is one side of the coin. On the other side of that coin, we can see an issue that may lead to disaster. People at the top of the tech world are extremely talented and are very aware of it. Such people don't often work well together. They expect special treatment and compete with each other for dominance. Because of this, many tech company CEOs don't want their "stars" to be involved in culture enhancement as it tends to add stress to the situation.

Yet, each of these experts brings immense value to the organization. Tech experts are in high demand and will be hired by competitors in the blink of an eye. Replacement cost is tremendously high due to the interview process and the delayed integration of a recruit into the team and training him or her to your organization's unique process. Seeing such a person go is like seeing money melt away. Thus, loyalty is critically important for tech companies. Not only does it reduce overall costs, it keeps knowledge in the organization.

At the same time, different teams of tech companies are often located far from each other. Members are sometimes even in different countries making collaboration more difficult. Building a strong culture of collaboration is vitally important in this situation. Teamwork should be taken very personally by every employee where he or she can explore their creativity and potential for growth.

Many very promising tech companies go bust because of a simple but vital mistake – they focus on what they can offer or produce instead of focusing on what potential customers or users really demand. As a result, their product looks fine, even interesting, but there is simply not enough customer interest. The reason lies in focusing culture on what can be done instead of what's needed. This leads to insufficient job satisfaction where employees question the value of their work on such projects.

Estate development and construction

One day, I had a nice relaxed chat with an old friend over a cup of coffee. He had recently changed jobs moving from leading a big retail chain to a large estate development company listed on the London Stock Exchange. I started to bombard him with questions about how he sees the specifics of corporate culture in estate development and construction with a fresh eye.

"Never rush and be patient as too much is at a stake. We are very conservative and contemplate our decisions for a long time, considering different factors." – was the first response of this mature CEO. Later, I received similar responses from leaders of the construction industry from around the world.

Developers hunt for high margin opportunities where operational costs are a secondary issue. They often face situations where the risk of doing something is much higher than the risk of waiting and hibernating. The lag in decision-making can be very long if the culture is focused mainly on securing the best contracts and most profitable locations and is fairly relaxed concerning efficiency.

Even though new technologies come up constantly, shareholders are mostly concerned with securing a steady cash flow and thus are careful with innovations.

Demographically, development and construction businesses are characterized by accommodating middle age and older employees with rich life and work experiences. The best businesses have experienced teams with a great deal of experience working together.

What can be improved in terms of culture in developers and construction companies? The main problem is that their learning curve is often too long which affects the implementation of necessary changes. It must be mentioned that these businesses have very high local influence and little if any global competition, reducing the need for change. It doesn't mean, however, that builders are not prepared for change if it is reasonable, sensible, and steady. However, those more responsive to learning and changing will outfight those who remain too conservative.

Universities

An old formula where universities were responsible for producing qualifications and diplomas is not attractive to the universities' stakeholders, specifically employers. Qualifications that involve little practical application of knowledge are not appealing to today's job market, which is more concerned with skills and competencies rather than writing ability.

It is understandable why universities are careful with innovations. There is too much at stake if something goes wrong for them and a history of success, which was gradually built over decades or even centuries, can be wiped out in a matter of days. However, in modern terms their old-fashioned culture often causes problems. In the vast majority of cases, such organizations are reactive in their action and not proactive as expected today. They follow the progress instead of advancing it. Universities rarely form active minds anymore. They qualify people instead of educating professionals capable of independent thought.

Preparing true professional is a field for which universities are not yet ready. However, this is a great opportunity that can be explored by mobilizing appropriate corporate culture at these knowledge-dependent organizations.

Universities and business schools have incredible potential to lead development by spearheading innovations and other creative approaches. What work and personal values graduates will bring to their future workplace depends on universities and business schools.

Every student, every graduate is the CEO of his own future. This understanding should be taught and nurtured before one gets into the actual workplace. If the students are taught to lead themselves well, they become better leaders when they reach the workplace. By creating a culture of teamwork, mutual support and growth, and creating value for others among students, universities will grow themselves enormously whether in teaching or in research.

Another problem of modern universities as knowledge-dependent organizations is that students and graduates, and their potential employers, have difficulties in seeing when knowledge taught will take effect or become practically useful. Would knowledge received in the university be utilized immediately or within a particular time, or in particular work circumstances? Often, the knowledge and techniques taught in the university can actually be lagging the demands of the marketplace.

Charities

Charities change the world by fulfilling their mission of lowering social barriers and helping those in need. Their power resides in social capital and, by definition, they must be masterful in networking, positive influence, and delivering value. Their job is to match the values of those donating with the needs of those suffering, which is an incredible valuable itself.

Charities need to sense social change just as any other type of business. They are always searching for supporters. This is never an easy task, particularly in financially difficult times. They strongly depend on constant feedback from donors and customers, acting as a bridge between them.

At the same time, working with limited budgets, they must employ volunteers and enthusiasts rather than professionals to do field work. Being effective, socially active, technologically savvy, open, sincere, and transparent is a job itself, and they often fail this basic test.

Far too many charities lack critical competence when it comes to effective collaboration. Instead of developing this competence and being open to collaborate with other charities, they often choose a path to competition with rivals over the same resources and donors which is the last thing they should do.

A charity's culture should be primarily focused on effective collaboration within its community and society at large. They must be effective for both donors and customers, and be socially visible through productive actions and deeds, all of which lower social barriers. Trust, professionalism, and transparency are crucial factors which enhance their social capital and support.

Attitude towards others: a matter of size or culture?

Company size matters a lot in determining how culture is cultivated, where its focus is, and how it is implemented. One can see this in thousands of different books, articles, and social media posts.

It seems to be clear that all companies demand strong internal culture. This is nothing new. In general, it is easier to maintain a strong culture in a small company compared to a large corporation. This is due to leaders having more direct and active interaction with employees, thus making it easier to control change processes and address problems as they arise.

However, we tend to look at culture in the context of company size as purely an internal issue, often neglecting the full influence that the culture itself has. Let's look at the differences between large and small businesses from a very peculiar angle – the way they do or do not treat partners as clients.

In April 2019, the British health food chain Holland & Barrett with 7,000 employees across 1,300 stores in the United Kingdom, Netherlands, Belgium, China, Hong Kong, India, Ireland, UAE, and eight other countries fell into a nation-wide scandal for "a purposeful culture of poor payment practices." Their small suppliers faced staggering delays in payment with about 60% of invoices not getting paid within the agreed time. Many of these small businesses went bankrupt.

Thousands and thousands of small business go bust or face sharp cuts in staff because of delays in payments from their larger partners. For instance, according to the UK Parliament report on Late Payments, Retentions and Government Procurement (2019), in the UK alone such late payments account for up to £225 billion per year. It should be mentioned that UK small businesses lose £60 billion per year because of bad debts where their US rivals experience $652 billion in bad debts per year.

While these companies refuse to pay on time and keep their business partners healthy and prosperous, they forget that some years ago they were small companies as well. Some started in a shed, some started with one small shop, and some survived because of their supportive partners. I don't think that the founders of Holland & Barret,

Alfred Slapps Barrett and Major William Holland, who started with one small grocery store in 1870 behaved in such a manner towards their suppliers. If they did, they would not have had a chance to survive and grow into a chain.

At the same time, the big guys like Kingfisher, Sony, and many others exhibit extreme diligence in paying smaller suppliers and supporting them with fair partnerships. So, where is the problem? Is it in size or in culture?

The truth is that attitude towards others is a matter of culture and has nothing to do with company size. Employees will behave towards partners according to their instructions, in a manner praised by their leaders, and absolutely in the same way as they are treated by the company.

Attitude towards others is a matter of culture and has nothing to do with company size

A company's internal culture is reflected in how it interacts with the rest of the world. It is critically important that these interactions are positive as any company is directly dependent on how it is seen by its customers and partners.

Leaders that cultivate culture of support, care, and respect to all partners and customers despite their size and status also nurture the numberless potentials for growth both inside and outside of their companies. Those leaders who treat people as silos are growing monsters who will eventually threaten to undermine the whole business.

Avoiding faux pas in a local context

National and local contexts of understanding corporate culture and how it's managed is probably one of the most critical factors. The same things could be understood and considered differently in different countries and even different parts of the same country.

Even in cases where a general consensus on the role and nature of corporate culture can be reached there are still a myriad of locally defined factors to be taken into account. There can be quite serious differences in understanding engagement and people's reaction to it, the role of families, rules of engagement and maintenance of work and social relationships, etc.

Engagement

The importance of engagement and its impact on overall organization's performance is indisputably critical. However, a management of engagement always demands an individual approach due to the mentality of management in a national context.

What happens in reality? For instance, according to the Gallup employee engagement report (2018), the highest level of engagement of 33% is demonstrated in the USA and is gradually growing. It can be attributed to the habit of hard work imprinted almost genetically in that country, high competition for jobs, and American's strong understanding of the fact that their company's success is tied the success of themselves and their families.

The British are more relaxed in this sense showing only a 17% level of engagement. To reach a higher level of engagement leaders should focus on three core aspects missing in the traditional British management style – respect for employees at all levels, employees' understanding of the importance of their roles in the organization, and opportunities for career growth. All three factors are important for leaders taking an interest in the professional growth of their employees. Promoting this new style of management has so far proven difficult.

Russia represents a much tougher case in terms of engagement. Statistics show that 19% of Russians are engaged in their work and enthusiastically support their companies. Then why are Russians not growing as other economies with above average engagement? In reality, statistics can't show the whole truth. Russians look at engagement as a Western fad which doesn't deserve much attention. However, the most serious problem lies much deeper. There are another 19% of employees who are actively resistant to active engagement. The main custom there is to position one's self as hard working, or being very busy, at least, but not being actually engaged. The Russian work traditions do not value enthusiasm. They consider it as foolish or swimming against the stream. Even those Russian companies that brag about their strong corporate culture are reluctant when it comes to care of employees, good customer service, or respect for partners. The mentality of managers, to rule and to give orders, is still strong in Russia and doesn't help much to engage people. Therefore, while doing business in this country leaders should focus on outfighting naysayers first and then stimulating actual engagement.

Attitude towards customers

If we consider that culture is critical in terms of customer service, then attitudes toward customers in different national domains reflect the natural presuppositions and biases of those areas. These biases, seemingly independent of the business actually are excellent indicators of how difficult it will be to affect any organizational change.

If you talk with a US supplier most likely you will get a response indicating everything is possible and the customer is (almost) always right. Your request will be strongly considered, and you will get what you want in most cases. Sounds like a paradise for those who know what they want, unless of course no one can actually deliver on those promises. US businesses are more inclined towards customers and generally more prepared to go the extra mile for them.

If you come with the same request to the UK you will face a different situation. They would not do much outside their area of specialization. We only do things we are accustomed to. I saw many times how Icelandic fish suppliers won competitions against their English rivals on English territory by being more flexible. On the positive side, the British will tell you that they can't deliver something beforehand and will explain to you in detail what you can get for your budget.

In Russia, a customer knows nothing or almost nothing and should be happy that we found time to talk with him. If we can't deliver our promises then it is purely the customer's fault. The customer is already wrong by definition and obliged to pay even when receiving nothing. Customer convenience is nonsense. Customer time and worries – why should they care?

Families as culture stakeholders

Families are culture stakeholders, and their roles are evident in any national context. However, it appears that the role of families in one culture can be more important in one than in another. For instance, in Azerbaijan, Georgia, Greece, Italy, France, Turkey, and many other countries, families are often more important than work. Their role and opinion must be seriously considered. Try to offer relocation to an Azerbaijani manager without talking to his parents and wife and see how far it will go.

Nationalities are different in the way work and social relationships are maintained, how people consider the purpose and logic of these ties, the nature of reciprocity and mutual support, and many other factors. This is not to mention that in many countries a normal expectation is that you must deliver some value before being accepted.

The ability to adapt to a local context is essential for any business thinking about global expansion. A nation's flavor of corporate culture is very dependent on local wisdom and the experience of previous generations and how people are accustomed to interacting. These local biases are dictated by what has been successful in local conditions, as well as the present state of development. Ignoring them means insulting people and their traditions, which is the last thing you want to do when trying to win hearts. Those who are not supported locally are more likely to face heavy resistance.

Differences as advantages

There are many variables to be considered while building a strong culture - different patterns of conducting business in different industries, different pace of evolution and drivers of performance in different types of organizations, national and local contexts, and strategies for different situations. Customers' expectations, the nature of competition, and the need for innovation should not be neglected even for a moment.

Talking about differences in culture is important. However, don't obsess over them. Differences will remain obstacles until you start using them as clues or bridges to opportunities and potentials to make people more satisfied. Focus on what is most important for people and build upon the commonalities.

Mastery in managing cultural differences in the Digital Era is only possible when the five factors of culture strengthening, flexibility, effective communication, teamwork, and diversity are considered as common and compulsory for your business.

Culture demands and anticipates real action which begins with a common understanding of that culture. Leaders, who act even with some mistakes and faults, generate enormous results. They talk to people, help them, and act on what they learn. Those who refuse to respect the many variables hurt not only themselves but the entire business.

Flexibility and preparedness for change is mandatory for cultivation of a productive culture regardless of the company specifics and context. The Digital Era is naturally disruptive and demands leaders' exhibit an ability to build a solid base and capacity for change. The main goal of any modern company is to encourage employees to make use of the many resources at their disposal to create new solutions that will better serve their customers.

Strong culture is a most effective platform for communicating meaning, motivating and energizing employees, and connecting hearts and minds. Effective communication is based on gratitude, strong belief in people and their abilities, respect, and seeing everyone as exceptionally valuable. Culture offers a unique instrument that gives every employee regardless of position, role, age, nationality, or experience the feeling of being a vitally important part of the organization.

Diversity is valuing everyone's differences. Or as Malcolm Stevenson Forbes said - "Diversity: the art of thinking independently together." This is a gift which helps to harmonize the Yin and Yang of any company and add extra strength to it. Diversity secures a strength and flexibility of culture by homogenizing talents, qualities, and views. Organizations that value diversity perform much better than rivals by viewing the differences in people as an opportunity to develop talents and qualities to help relate to the largest possible customer base.

Teamwork is the hallmark of a strong culture. Whether a culture is solid and represents a single united force or fragmented and difficult to manage reflects the degree of teamwork in a company. It depends on the members' emotional attachment, interdependency of their roles, a sense of belonging, and other factors that will be discussed in the next chapter in greater detail.

Practical tips

- Never try to duplicate the nature of another kind of business as it may lead to conflict within your company. What is good for one business would not be effective for another one.

- Every employee must be treated as a Human. People will open their hearts if their needs, desires, personal and professional perspectives are considered first. A leader must win hearts first and professional enthusiasm will follow.

- Talking with people as workforce units is a sure way to build a wall of defensiveness and resistance, as it is a strong sign of disrespect.

- Culture must be attuned to the purpose and goals of each organization.

- Communicating culture in all types of businesses and national contexts is crucial. Every message should be weighed against four factors – simplicity, clarity, consistency, and attention to people.

- Don't offend or even insult people by ignoring their local cultural differences. Always look out for local habits and practices that can be used effectively or even adapted to your company. You might learn something.

- Cultural differences obscure enormous opportunities for development and growth. Explore them thoroughly instead of worrying about them.

Chapter Eight

A SECRET SAUCE FOR STRONG CULTURE

Culture can make a business go around and grow stronger. But, there are three ingredients that can double its effectiveness. These three ingredients make a secret sauce that any leader should use in cultivating a strong culture regardless of industry or national context. Even a negative culture that preys off people's dissatisfaction turns into a gentle caring giant after tasting this sauce.

How to prepare it? We need three main ingredients – overlapping roles, every employee being a culture investor, and making culture a verb of acting and caring for others.

To start with, take a bowl full of employees' understanding of how their role and expectations.

Add a good portion of willingness to invest their own effort into the support and encouragement of others.

Mix thoroughly.

While making this mixture keep adding a sense of action until the mixture rises.

Every ingredient must be organic, fresh, and prepared in accordance with the specific needs of an organization. Let's look at every ingredient in detail.

Overlapping roles

What everyone's role is in terms of corporate culture defines how people support each other and allows them to realize the impact of their work on others, colleagues, customers, and the organization as a whole. This is not a mere job description. A job description is necessary, but it can restrict an employee's vision of the inner life of an organization as one single body.

We need employees thinking and acting outside of their mental boxes instead of standing separately as independent workforce units. Otherwise, the culture will remain fragmented and unable to realize its full potential.

To start, ask top managers to do a simple exercise writing no more than ten to twelve short answers for the following five questions. Let them grasp the full meaning and importance of understanding the interdependency of roles and what impact their work has on others.

- What is my role for the organization?
- What is my role for colleagues and peers from all other departments?
- What is my role in satisfying the customer?
- What is my role for subordinates or apprentices?
- What is my role for superiors?

For instance, the role of an Operations Director can be described in the following manner.

- What is my role for the organization? Operations are concerned with everyone's efficiency whether on an individual or a company level. My role is to lower all transaction costs and eradicate all existing and potential frictions in processes and so improve performance.
- What is my role for colleagues and peers from all other departments? I am a tailor stitching all elements together making them perfectly fit. My role is to coordinate all

activities and make sure that employees from all functions and departments interact in the most effective way.

- What is my role in satisfying the customer? My role is to make sure that a product is delivered on time with the expected quality. My role is to increase the value for the customer through the efficiency of internal and external processes.

- What is my role for subordinates or apprentices? My role for direct and indirect subordinates is in leading them, sharing experience, helping them to grow, showing areas for improvement, and bearing full responsibility for them. I am a member of the team as well.

- What is my role for superiors? My role for superiors is to make sure that the company's strategy implementation and execution of roles and duties by my subordinates and me personally contribute to individual and corporate growth.

Top managers and executives should demonstrate a clear understanding of their roles and extended responsibilities after completing this task. This will allow them to stretch their vision of their roles as far as the most remote boundaries of an organization's influence.

Employees should perform the same exercise. Leaders of all levels should help employees with this task. Every newcomer should be helped with understanding his or her role at the very beginning of the adaptation period. The aim is to ingrain in employees a clear and meaningful understanding of who are they in the organization.

Keep in mind that there are many possible answers to these questions. The goal is to help everyone in the organization to get a better understanding of their roles.

It should be considered that with the change of the organization's goals, the meaning of roles may change, necessitating a revisiting of everyone's role description.

Everyone is an investor

A strong culture is not about me but about what I do for others. Strong culture demands daily investments in terms of time to cement meaningful relationships, effort to understand people, and care for them. Every leader must sponsor and invest, contributing empathy, encouragement, and support to fellow employees and customers.

Corporate relationships are channels that transfer mutual effort and support, through which cultural investments are facilitated. Those who are aware of how to make the relations deep and meaningful win the game in modern business.

Culture depends on genuine support, mutual engagement, and empathy, where fake sentiment can't mask the inconsistency and negativity of toxic culture. Here are six questions that employees should ask themselves on a regular basis that will help to understand the importance of doing something positive and valuable for others:

- What do I actually do for people? What is my role in investing in others?
- What difference do I make for people in the short (6 - 12 months) and long (1-3 years) run?
- How I am supported by my people?
- How can I make it easier for my colleagues to ask each other for help?
- What potentials for enhancing relationships can I see?
- What do customers feel after dealing with our culture as external consumers and unbiased judges?

Let's look at these questions closely through the lens of cultivating a productive culture.

There is tremendous power behind the wisdom of reciprocity – help others and expect help in return, listen to what people need and share with them what you have or know, by being an example in supporting others.

Individual resources grow through expanding collaboration with others. At the same time, an enhanced understanding of culture and its potential among employees directly influences a culture's strength and productiveness, thus, making employees culturally savvy pays back enormously.

Becoming important for others, growing as a person and growing professionally as a cultural investor is another essential trait for navigating the digital age.

In fact, by helping employees to become culturally savvy and facilitating mutual success, leaders gain a strong platform for maintaining culture which pays back an organization and employees with enormous personal and professional growth and satisfaction.

Culture is a verb of acting and caring

Russians have an old saying – we bridle a carriage slowly but ride it very fast. Today it is very different, Russians tend to laugh about themselves – we are bridling a carriage slowly, not riding at all, and unbridling it quickly. This reminds me of a situation that can often be seen in many offices where leaders are actively engaged in ongoing discussions about the importance of cultivating productive culture but do nothing about it in terms of action.

Culture demands everyday action. A leader is an action pacesetter. In this sense, doing is not just declaring or proclaiming. Don't waste time with cheap talk, start doing and the resulting dynamic culture will offer a return above any expectations.

Think of action as a language. For instance, the main expression of love is giving and doing. Giving is what one does for others, caring is the action itself. Positive culture revitalizes people by enhancing their capacity to care for and think of others. Understanding means placing effort into absorbing and analyzing knowledge and information and making it practically applicable. Gaining understanding is acting as well and a prerequisite of efficient and timely action.

I was talking with my friend Peter, a retired nuclear submarine commander, about how actions are communicated in difficult situations. "As a Commander, I give tens of orders per minute in certain situations, and some of them may be relayed to a few teams simultaneously. Whatever I say, whatever I want my crew to do, I finish my order with the clear call for action. These and these valves – activate now; these and these valves and locks – shut down now; standby and get ready for such and such action – now!" Peter continued his explanation further with "Acting precisely and consciously is mandatory for turning a crew into one body, one extremely effective team, where one stands for all and all stand for one. You can't achieve such conditions by talking only but only through action with all crew members being involved. Let people understand what they are expected to do and get into an imprinted habit of immediate acting."

Continuing the military metaphor, I should stress that culture demands acting from A to Z, and from the first to the last moment of engagement. In corporate terms, it means executing duties and obligations to others as a decent resident of the culture until the last day of employment, not relaxing with your feet up a few weeks before resigning.

Practical tips

- Culture is a beauty that we create together by supporting and acting for others enthusiastically.

- Simplicity and clear understanding help people to preserve the authenticity of a culture where overcomplicating things leads to a mess.

- Leaders' reluctance and inactivity act like rotten or out-of-date ingredients that will spoil every delicacy on a culture's menu.

Part Three

LEADERSHIP

Leadership is a management function that connects people, finds and explores opportunities that define and secure a prosperous future for employees and customers. It is about problem-solving and finding the best ways out of problems that distance businesses from their customers. Leadership is about how to contribute to people's growth, knowing what to do next, and securing their prosperous future.

Leaders' duties and tasks are getting more and more complicated every day. Don't be afraid of complicated tasks or complex projects. Be afraid of initially poor leadership. It will ruin any business much quicker than you think. It can damage people and their lives dramatically.

No one is insured against mistakes. Leadership is an everyday challenge. Occasionally, the reality of business will hit hard. Stand up when knocked down and continue the fight. A leader who fights for people despite adversity is already winning.

Chapter Nine

LEADERSHIP: VISION, PREPARATION, ACTION

A common assumption is that anyone motivated can be a leader. However, it takes more than motivation. Being a leader requires a great deal of knowledge, the drive to continually improve, and a genuine desire to serve others.

Many believe that they can wake up and miraculously become a good leader because they are motivated and wish to be at the top of the game. Leaders unskilled in people management, even those highly motivated, are bound to lose and hurt others in the process rather than generate a profit. Motivation without vision, leadership competencies, and knowledge only increase the number of highly motivated idiots. Unfortunately, we are witnessing too many such cases. Motivation that comes only from external factors like profit and prestige is always short-term. Motivation should come from within, resulting in a strong flow of energy and desire that will build upon and expand pre-existing competencies.

Internal motivation springing from a clear vision can help inspire others to find their own motivation. External motivation without self-discovery is an artificial form of encouragement which only reveals those desperately aiming to get into a power position at any cost.

Leadership is an extremely difficult duty. It is not easy even for genuinely natural leaders. Every leader I know has had the experience of overcoming their leadership fear at the beginning of their career and regularly felt the pressure of their responsibilities since then.

Whatever roles a leader takes, they are all great in vision, preparation for new challenges, and acting for people.

Vision

Vision is a divine gift entrusted to those who will use it to empower others. Vision is a concentration of desires, dreams, potentials, and possibilities. A vision pushes people not just to do more but to do more than they think they are capable of.

Vision is transcendental and not easy to fully grasp, despite hearing it almost every day. This triggered even more of my interest to explain the nature of vision based on the experience of many leaders with whom I discussed this phenomenon – CEOs of big companies, serial entrepreneurs, creators of unique software, and many others. Every single person with whom I spoke viewed vision differently. Yet, six properties of a strong vision remained constant. These six core properties of a strong vision are stimulus, scale, scanning, spotlight, simplicity, and excitement. The paradigm of vision can be expressed in 5S&E model.

Checking against this paradigm allows for evaluating your vision at any stage of your leadership journey.

Stimulus - Vision reflects the highest purpose of leadership – purposeful acting for and with people. Vision should include the actual benefits for those affected by it. This passion for people must include to differing degrees, employees, customers, leaders themselves, employees' families, and society at large.

A main stimulus of vision is people and care of their needs. Ask a simple question - who would benefit from your vision and be passionate supporters of it in return? As vision is meant to be about people's future, it can't be built without them. If a vision is not formed around people and their needs, then it is not vision but personal ambition.

Scale - Vision should be of great breadth and depth and potential for extension at later stages. Vision never leads to or accepts a dead end. It shows multiple potentials for expansion. In other words, good vision is always scalable.

To be able to scale the vision one should maintain an appropriate cognitive distance from it. This allows seeing the broader picture while keeping the important details in sight. Standing too close only allows one to see the details while losing the whole picture. Standing too far means losing important details from which the vison is created. In the first case, one loses the whole meaning of the vision for nothing. In the second case, the vision becomes detached from reality.

It is also important to consider that a leader transfers vision to customers through his or her organization and its people. Vision must be delivered to customers. Thus, every team member must be customer focused.

Scanning - Watch for the signs and clues in pursuit of your vision while choosing the best ways to success. They will be easy to follow if the vision is strong. A visionary is a futurist who sees the signs on his way to success. If one will keep his mind and eyes open, then those signs are always around in different forms – words of encouragement, expressions of real need from strangers, and answers to critical questions coming from unexpected perspectives.

This is not a joke. Think for a moment that a strong vision is usually associated with believers with strong imagination. Why? They are excellent at spotting tiny signs of unusual opportunities. Attention to these signs and clues helps leaders to spot opportunities while crafting the most effective path to success.

Spotlight - Vision assumes responsibility, immediate and extended. The greater the vision then the greater the responsibility for its impact on people's lives, and for what legacy will be left afterwards.

However, this huge responsibility comes with incredible opportunities, the kinds of opportunities only available to pioneers. Think for a moment – responsibility with opportunity. It may be intimidating to take on all that responsibility, but it will reward you in return. Thus, vision means significance of opportunities.

Simplicity – Vision involves elegant thinking about complicated things. Great vision is genuinely easy to understand and never complicated. It is like as a breath of fresh air.

The simpler the vision in its core meaning, the easier it can be shared with employees, customers, and partners, and thus, easier to scale inside and outside an organization. Simplicity of vision allows it to be shared easily with and between employees, from employees to customers, and among customers.

Complication is the enemy of great vision. If things are too complicated and too difficult to grasp, then most likely this is not a real vision but an overcomplicated puzzle. No one can solve complex problems for people without attracting supporters and developing empathy on a big scale if the vision is too complicated. Too much complexity simply turns people off.

Excitement - Strong vision emanates from the face of its possessor. Strong vision is always accompanied by excitement. Actually, vision is a strong emotion itself.

If someone tells you about his great vision with a sad or boring face, then most likely he is lying to himself and others. Such a person might have a goal but not a vision.

If we assume the five elements of strong vision as stimulus are in place, then excitement is there. In other words, E (Excitement) =5S.

Do you remember how you felt the first time you solved a difficult problem? Having a vision is like that, but on a much greater scale, whether industry, national, or global in scale. Vision is accompanied with strong confidence in achieving the goal and adding value to many people. This brings happiness which is difficult to contain, happiness that is infectious.

Why do leaders need vision? Vision defines and explains why and where effort should be focused. At the same time, there is no opportunity to add value to people without a clear vision of how it will be added and in which form. Leadership is blind without vision.

Vision is normally created by a single person but quickly becomes the property of many. No one can accomplish something great on his or her own. Vision is what attracts the people needed to make it a reality. It becomes a force driving many to a common goal. As the vision grows into a reality, it attracts an ever-growing pool of supporters.

Vision fully occupies the mind of its possessor. It pushes out all issues that will negatively affect its achievement. This is why visionaries are incredibly effective as leaders.

Preparation

Taking a leadership role means being prepared to grow by constantly answering important questions – Why should I become better? Why should I change all the time? Why should I accept greater responsibility? Why should I get prepared for every stage of my career and every new project doing so again and again?

Every stage of a leader's career, whether working on a new project or going through a radical stage of development demands a fresh new start. Each stage requires a different vision with different goals. The leader must be prepared to reinvent himself to meet fresh challenges.

Analogically speaking, we can say that achieving success is like reaching a new rank in martial arts. At the highest level is the black belt. It is a confirmation of the many years one has challenged oneself, trained hard, and climbed from learner to master.

Like martial arts, leadership demands thoughtful preparation and constant challenge. We accept this in many areas of life. To excel at a sport or art requires dedication and sacrifice. The sciences as well require constant learning to remain at the top of a given field. A leader who does not adopt this mind set eventually fails and contributes to the failure of everyone he or she is responsible for. Deluding oneself into the belief that you are already good enough will lead to disaster.

There are five critical elements of preparation that should be considered – studying a new field, learning, psychological and emotional readiness, growing inner excellence, and growing confidence and credibility.

Novelty

How many times have you found yourself in a completely new life and work environment? For most of us, the answer is – hundreds of times. Most of us can cite relocating to a new city, changing jobs, or going to a top-notch gala event for the first time.

When stepping into a new environment, it is absolutely normal for everyone to study and to note what is different and compare it to what is already familiar. We look for opportunities to use our qualities, skills, and experience in this new environment.

While studying a new environment, we need to engage all our senses to clear the fog of uncertainties, settle comfortably, and learn the best use of the new conditions. This requires us to be quick on our feet and be able to quickly read people and situations, especially when entering a new leadership role.

Learning

Professional and personal learning and growth is a treasure in itself. Learning means growth and transformation. Learning allows us to understand our goals and how to get there. Without learning, we can't become who we want to be.

A good leader is unique. There are no two leaders with identical qualities and competencies. One of those differences is their capacity to determine what needs to be learned and how quickly. What is common is that all good leaders put enormous effort into learning, every day, in every condition. The modern leader should learn every day, whether about the financial side of business, industry developments, every facet of the ever-globalizing and fast-paced competition, or psychology for a better understanding of people.

Enhanced understanding of people has become a priority in learning due to the enormously growing importance of individuals in every organization. No leader can help people grow without understanding them.

Understanding of and being connected to people with their needs and desires and being connected with them is the highest goal of the modern leader. While reaching this goal, a leader explores people's potentials, arms them with important meanings, and defines the destination. This is a ladder the leader builds for himself and his employees. In this sense, learning means growing and expanding your capacities and competencies for others. This inner expansion allows one to see people's potentials.

I recommend learning for a couple of hours every day. This will prepare you to meet the unexpected challenges of tomorrow.

Psychological and emotional readiness

Inexperienced leaders often face a staggering problem that threatens to break them. They mainly rely on hard skills and dismiss the importance of soft skills, completely neglecting the psychological and emotional pressure under which all leaders act.

A leader's growth is limited by psychological and emotional unpreparedness. The larger the business, the greater responsibility, which leads to greater psychological and emotional challenges.

No one tells young prospective leaders or MBA students that top management work is psychological. This is similar to a situation where one climbs a high peak (growth) with a heavy backpack (responsibilities and duties) in harsh conditions (everyday problems and issues) while needing to motivate and encourage a team, a team that might be unwilling. The team might urge you to take a long break or give up and return to a warm shelter. This is tremendous psychological and emotional pressure from people you need to rely on for support, on top of pressure from many external factors. Sound tough? Now think of the emotional pressure on the CEO of a large company with thousands of employees and stockholders monitoring every move.

The leader cannot allow employees to see him overwhelmed by that pressure. They won't believe in a vision promoted by someone who is visibly worried and stressed out.

Growing inner excellence

Leaders lead by example, inspiring others with their own conviction and energy. Leaders build their own selves, so they can better serve others. Leaders also continually improve their own understanding of the current environment. This involves constant inner processing of facts and ideas to best implement the vision.

No one is perfect but getting better and growing in excellence is a leader's responsibility. This requires life-long mental training. The process is often invisible from the outside, particularly for those who associate leadership with superficial attributes like high income, a nice office, and other perks.

As the leader develops, he or she is better able to fight doubts, confront anxiety, keep the inner spirit up, and learn from mistakes. This demands inspiration, creativity, and relentlessness in finding unconventional ways to make employees and customers satisfied. Also, the leader must be mentally flexible. Flexibility is the mark of a leader with a well-trained mind.

Confidence and credibility

People evaluate a leader much the way they would a survival guide. They want to see professionalism, confidence, and credibility. The leader with confidence in his own competencies and abilities is worth ten hesitant ones. The credible leader stands above the competition, drawing others to himself.

No one can build a future without confidence. Knowing what to do and how to do it, with confidence and competence, is a must for a professional leader.

Confidence in a way means defeating yourself over and over. It means defeating your fears and anxieties, your tendency to procrastinate. This isn't possible in the long term if you are only doing it for yourself. The good leader must build himself for others and not just for himself or even to defeat the competition. Confidence comes when one is sure that he or she fulfills and even surpasses his or her commitments to customers and employees.

Lolly Dascal (The Leadership Gap, 2017) clearly asserted that "Confidence believes you are able. Competence knows you are able." This combination of confidence and competence with added effort allows people to add extraordinary value to the organization.

The leader must be credible, exhibiting consistency in words, actions, and deeds. What is more important, kindness and attention to people directly affect the leader's credibility. People want their leader to be authentic.

Acting

Leading means constant engagement. Engagement means being fully committed, with full concentration on developing employees to help achieve the organization's goals as well as their own.

The leader's key performance indicators (KPIs) in terms of acting are a strong culture with engaged employees, a growing number of happy and satisfied customers, and discovering new horizons to strive for and grow the people and the organization. These KPIs are always dynamic and forward thinking.

Leadership actions mean solving inefficiencies in the processes of human interaction and making a difference for people every day. This is based on the irresistible will to act, turning vision and words into real deeds.

What is important for leaders to consider beside their usual duties? Every leader should consider three critical factors which may affect effective engagement - influence, connecting people, and overcoming resistance. Let's talk about these three elements of engagement.

Influence

Vision is a gift that must be multiplied. The ability to multiply that gift strongly depends on the leader's ability to influence. The greater the vision, the greater the demand for strong and far-reaching influence.

There is no leadership without the ability to influence and inspire people to engage in action beyond themselves to channel thoughts and effort in one direction.

Influence is a manageable power with a multidimensional nature. There are six points that should be considered while turning it into an effective instrument of growth.

- The strength of influence is defined by the energy a leader pours into people and how they become charged with confidence, positivity, and enthusiasm.

- There is no such thing as remote influence. A leader's influence depends on his closeness to people. Influence is about being with people, walking them to a destination, not just pointing in a direction.

- A leader becomes influential and powerful by being simple. Influence is a matter of simplicity. It is always difficult to transmit complicated things without losing the exact meaning and important details.

- Influence depends on the leader's warmness, benevolence, insightfulness, authenticity, intelligence, and ability to handle multiple points of view.

- Influence is about building a base of believers and supporters. No one can achieve something huge on his own. By expanding his influence, a leader gains greater human and social resources allowing for greater progress towards clearly defined goals.

- Influence can't depend on old methods and achievements. It must be consistently stimulated with something new.

Connecting people

Paulo Coelho (2006) said in his famous novel *The Zahir*, "The most important thing in all human relationships is conversation, but people don't talk anymore, they don't sit down to talk and listen. They go to the theatre, the cinema, watch television, listen to the radio, read books, but they almost never talk. If we want to change the world, we have to go back to a time when warriors would gather around a fire and tell stories."

Can one who is not creating a flourishing environment where people interact effectively be considered a leader? Would you work under the command of such a person and prosper?

Leaders connect people. Think of this simple slogan as one of the leader's main roles. Acting means merging people and being diligent in helping employees and customers to become happy, satisfied, and mutually effective while achieving the organization's goals.

The leader acts as an architect for the organization, building it as a collective of mutually affected people working for a common vision. The leader is taking all the pressure and connecting and supporting different elements of the structure.

Connecting people allows everyone involved to equally access all available resources such as competencies, qualities, and growing potentials needed for achieving new heights in personal and professional growth.

We are well into the age of interconnectivity whether in the workplace or in relations with customers. Leaders assume responsibility for creating a business as a microcosm where people organically and effectively interact and communicate. The past addiction to hierarchy separated teams, and often led to inconsistency in management.

The greatest value is always produced by well-connected people, not by separated individuals. The leader acts to connect people quickly and efficiently adding value to people and the company as well.

However, people are not born with the advanced skills necessary to unify desire and effort. Plus, modern social technologies can have a negative impact in terms of disconnecting people when used inappropriately. People need to be coached by their leader as to how to interact effectively, complement each other, and enhance their social qualities.

Overcoming resistance

Leadership is about overcoming resistance every day. Getting rid of the old and dated while preparing minds for something new, eradicating negativity, and implementing needed change is never easy.

Staying in rigid paradigms is like living in a bubble with limited resources. In the end, you can only observe the outside world without having any effect on it. The ability to overcome resistance and leave an old paradigm depends greatly on the extent a leader can ignore odds, stupidity, and naysayers on the way to implementing change. It demands a great deal of patience, persistence, focus, and mastery in sensing people's needs.

Overcoming resistance and implementing change also demands a perfect sense of timing. Implementing change too quickly leads to forcing people to change before they are ready. In this case, people blindly follow instructions, burying their doubts until they grow to a point they can't be concealed. The result is that the change may fail or even degrade the organization's culture. Spending too much time on implementing change allows doubts to redevelop, leading to rehashing the same issues over and over. In such cases, the leader has failed to find the right arguments to break down the old paradigm and motivate people to accept and implement the new vision.

Thus, a great part of engagement is about challenging people's inner doubts and helping them out of their mental bubbles. All great leaders exhibit this behavior. Whether we recall such famous political or business leaders as Nelson Mandela, Bill Gates, Charles Schwab, Howard Schultz, or many others who change the world, they are all masters of overcoming resistance.

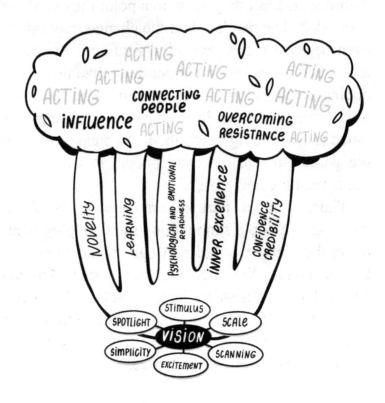

Conclusions

The number of businesses is growing daily and as such the demand for leaders with vision will grow exponentially.

Leadership is not about being employed by a company but serving employees and customers. The real leader serves people, and not his or her own ambitions. In this sense, modern leadership is about serving people and adding value to them every day.

Those who earn the respect of others through hard work, positive engagement, and exhibiting genuine concern for customers and employees are those who rise to the top and achieve results that can change the world.

Practical tips

- Modern leadership is a privilege belonging to those skilled in serving people with a positive impact on their future. Be careful – seeing your people succeed is addictive.

- Help people grow and they will make you a better leader.

- Setting a low bar doesn't help increase efficiency, enhance an outcome, or gain supporters. Raise a bar high and it will attract more supporters than you can imagine.

- A bad leader is like a shadow over a team's success. A good leader always cares for people, in good and bad days, in clear and cloudy weather. A good leader understands success is a collective achievement.

- The world is growing, leaving those with a lack of vision behind. The gap between yesterday and tomorrow is widening every day for them.

- The future is a harsh judge of what we do today. Today gives us a chance to change the future for the good of others.

- Leadership requires action and results. Those hiding behind intentions have no role in leadership.

- Servant leadership puts the needs of others above all. Today it is a competitive advantage of a few - tomorrow it will be the norm for all.

- Leaders serve both employees and customers, acting for the good of all. A leader is the customers' ambassador inside of an organization and employees' ambassador to customers.

Chapter Ten

FOURTEEN COMMON PROBLEMS AND DISEASES

There are problems that distance a business from its customers and limit its ability to satisfy them as fully as possible. Problems like those increase costs, lower performance level, restrict growth, and can kill the business if not dealt with.

Business can't and shouldn't be ideal. Organizations are dynamic in their nature and exist in an ever-changing environment. Everything in organizational life revolves around customers demand, which is dynamic itself, making things even more complicated.

Finally, businesses have pathologies, disorders, and diseases as humans do. An organization can't perform at its best and be profitable when limited by pathologies and diseases. Serious problems that threaten a company's existence usually begin from simple organizational diseases which can be treated if correctly diagnosed.

Approaches and methods effective yesterday may not be effective today and may even be damaging tomorrow. Therefore, mistakes and problems from the past may be costly in the future. In other words, taking pills without changing bad habits and adapting to new conditions isn't a proper treatment and only makes life more difficult.

Roots of problems

Problems are the result of human behavior. Customers or the company itself are not a source of problems. Whether it's incompetent leadership, negative culture, or poor execution of duties, the cause of problems resides in people inside the business.

While working with different companies I noticed that in a vast majority of cases the previous reports did not recognize actual problems and causes but were merely costly exercises in paper pushing. These formal reports are costly and meaningless wastes of time and a drag on the company.

Unfortunately, too many leaders assume that the company will manage itself instead of taking control over it on a daily basis. Many companies repeat the same old mistakes – overestimating the strength of their brand, not adapting to change, restricting innovation, and not understanding customers. Those not learning and innovating for the customers' good will die despite their size and market share. This happened with Kodak, Blockbuster, Nokia, BlackBerry, Xerox, Toys R Us, and many others. We should thank them for what they did and the lessons we've learned from their faults.

Besides making strategic decisions and trying to be purely rational, leaders must act as organizational developers and diagnosticians who take care of their companies in the long-term. They must use their best abilities and senses in solving problems and taking action. While listening to the whole body of an organization or each part of it, leaders of all levels are required to make balanced decisions that are the most appropriate for a particular situation and will remain sustainable.

Seeing good in bad

It is critically important for businesses to realize what problems they have and solve them as soon as possible. The famous American Clergyman, Roy L. Smith, once said - "The successful man is the one who finds out what is the matter with his business before his competitors do."

We tend to forget that every success story begins with solving a problem. Overcoming problems and learning from them paves the road to success. Problems always have at least one solution, particularly when we concentrate on the answer and don't panic over possible consequences. It depends on how we look at them – as something feasible to solve if structured and understood or something threatening.

It is no secret that problems help to explore opportunities. For instance, Ivan Vaughan, a psychologist, boyhood friend of John Lennon and schoolmate of Paul McCartney was diagnosed with Parkinson's in 1977. He didn't give in to this disease, which strongly affects the functioning of the brain and nervous system, and searched tirelessly for a cure. Ivan wrote a book "Ivan: Living with Parkinson's Disease" which was published in 1986.

He was writing while on levodopa, which is an amino acid used to increase dopamine concentrations in the treatment of Parkinson's disease. It helped his thoughts flow freely, as he shares his fascinating, even thrilling experience. When the treatment stopped Ivan used the mind's slow motion as an ideal opportunity for editing and highlighting risky passages. Ivan Vaughan's case proves that opportunity stands behind every problem, even Parkinson's.

Fourteen Most Common Pathologies and Diseases

Corporate problems can be structurally viewed as pathologies and diseases. In general, pathologies are imprinted initially whereas diseases are picked up during the life of a company and can be typological, neurological, and general in nature.

Problems are the result of human behavior. Customers or the company itself are not the source of problems. Whether incompetent leadership, negative culture, or poor execution of duties, the cause of problems resides in people inside the business.

Corporate problems are usually the result of the leaders' action or inaction. Problems can be rooted in leaders' poor understanding of their organizations' nature and purpose, and not understanding business as a system of caring for customers. Thus, corporate problems have psychological roots which should be mainly addressed to the leaders.

I discussed some of these typical problems before in my book *Organisational Anatomy* (2016). This chapter offers a revised and extended discussion of fourteen common and harmful pathologies and diseases.

Typological disorders

Typological properties dictate the need for a clear understanding of archetypes and their specific characteristics and roles and influence how effectively a company's potential is used.

Loss of self-awareness

Loss of self-awareness manifests when an organization uses the pattern of resource utilization relevant to another archetype, size, or operational principle, and by doing so ignores its own advantages and inappropriately uses non-specific and undeveloped properties. In simple words, it is a case where a knowledge-dependent organization such as a bank acts as a supermarket, expecting unrealistic results and sympathy from customers.

Any company is a locus of exceptional power if formed and managed in accordance with its imprinted properties and purpose. Otherwise, it loses effectiveness dramatically. A dog is not born to climb trees. A company with such a disorder performs at 30-50% of its full potential which is not enough to succeed in the modern competitive world. It loses focus and wastes energy and resources. This disorder can kill the company in time.

An organization can't change its archetype with simple cosmetic surgery. It would be against its constitution to incorporate inappropriate processes, culture, patterns of relationships, and management styles. Therefore, if an organization is willing to get involved in other kinds of business, it will be logical to establish separate entities which will take care of the new ventures. If the organization has already fallen into the trap, then it should conduct structural revisions to restore and revitalize the imprinted core activity, making sure that it becomes pure again.

All activities must be checked against archetypal properties and roles every three to six months. The aim of such revision is to see whether the company advances customers in its activities or has left its path. All non-related activities must be slashed without regret. I witnessed a case where a medium-size food processor rose from the ashes like a phoenix after such a revision and almost doubled production.

The Napoleon complex

The size of a company defines the scale and scope of organizational potentials as well as operations. It also defines the need for relevant structural properties. This is related to organizations that lack awareness of their own boundaries, which makes processes quite costly, inappropriate, and excessive. In such cases, an organization carries extra weight and will suffer eventually for not reaching the anticipated result. Such a problem can be viewed as a "Napoleon complex."

Most often a Napoleon complex can be seen in small companies when they attempt to incorporate elements, processes, policies, and functions typical for larger organizations. It happens largely because of top management with previous corporate experience not understanding small business well or owners copying large companies' processes at high costs. However, I noticed recently this disorder in an international corporation with at least two big dysfunctional departments whose activities were having no impact on value except adding extra cost. Those departments seem to exist only for the leader's ego.

Being a lean organization means being structured in accordance with its size and market share. If a company doesn't know its boundaries, then most likely it will lose touch with customers, experience bloated production, and have difficulty with market positioning. This disorder costs a company its customers because of increased formalities and expenses which a small business can't cope with.

What is the solution? The answer is simple – realistically evaluate a company's properties and capacities.

Goal perplexity

Leaders define the goals of their business. Organizations without clear goals are purposeless. Such organizations don't know how effective they are and eventually lose sight of why they exist in the first place.

The good news is that goal perplexity is not a very serious problem if the company doesn't need customers and a business is established for the sake of keeping its founders being busy. This problem can be observed in start-ups which can't clearly articulate their services to customers and so, streamline the effective production processes. They quickly fail and leave nothing behind except bills and disappointment.

Goal perplexity happens when leaders have difficulties with setting goals, resulting in big problems. It rocks a company from side to side, from one extreme to another, unconsciously picking up good and bad habits from its rivals. Even a mature company can face this disorder, particularly when rewriting strategic goals, or facing big but empty changes. A company may be infected with goal perplexity when experiencing a conflict of shareholders and top management interests as they pull it in different directions. Also, a company can be stuck, unable to offer a new product range while the old one has lost its appeal to customers as happened with GoPro.

GoPro is not a one-off case. Large companies with 10,000-15,000 and even more employees without clearly defined goals are fairly common. For instance, I dealt recently with a company with direct investments of about $100 million and is still suffering because of the lack of clear goal.

While facing this problem, the organization becomes an easy target for competitors. It weakens market position as customers are not eager to support such a company. The best talent leaves rather than face a negative culture and the forthcoming collapse.

Competitor's dependency syndrome

Competition is based on willingness to compete. However, it seems that managers do not always realize that competition can be useful. Yet is can have a dangerous side effect. Very often, competitors tend to copy others' behavior, eventually leading them to patterned thinking and similar actions blindly following the competitor's market behavior.

Such an approach causes a psychological dependency leading to the development of competitors' dependency syndrome. Businesses affected by this syndrome are like little kids on the school playground fighting over the same ball with plenty of others being available. Products are replicated by similar products; discounts follow similar competitor's discounts; customer engagement programs become all too similar.

Copying competitors does not create industry or market leaders but rather reveals weakness. Copying the competitor's actions only works to the point that one of the competitors fail due to exhaustion rather than exploring its own potentials.

This syndrome is harmful to both company and customers. The company loses its uniqueness and limits its own potentials. Customers do not profit either.

Think of the wise Oscar Wilde's advice - "Be yourself; everyone else is already taken."

Neurological diseases

Both nervous systems, central and peripheral, can be affected by neurological diseases that negatively influence the internal and external activities of organizations. Like the other corporate diseases these distance the company from its customers. Such problems can be seen in the form of thrombosis, tie atrophy, muteness, incoordination syndrome, muteness, and cross syndrome.

Thrombosis

An effective company is characterized by the easy and natural flow of resources. Unfortunately, many companies face the locking of resources somewhere in the midst of Byzantine processes. This is known as thrombosis. This disease limits access, gain, and effective processing of all resources, including information. Resources and assets caught between departments and functions work against profit and increase governance and processing costs as well as reducing the production rate.

Think of a truck with fresh meat waiting for hours to be unloaded at the supermarket's gate without any valid reason. When unloaded, the products are not quickly placed on shelves. The responsible staff is hiding somewhere, taking long coffee breaks, or using silly excuses not to do their work. I saw similar cases in fish factories in Norway, supermarkets in the UK and Russia, and airports in Germany.

Thrombosis is a voluntary or involuntary delay, or blockage of resources, which increases costs and negatively influences overall performance. Thrombosis can also be seen occurring in a number of processes simultaneously where many small problems lead to serious underperformance.

Resulting from underperformance and even a purposeful sabotage of relevant departments, thrombosis causes further inconsistencies and losses in performance. This is the result of purely unprofessional behavior that may cost a company up to 30% efficiency and even more if it goes unnoticed.

No customer can be attracted by unprofessional staff and absurdly expensive products. In this sense, it is up to the company's leaders to decide what to do with employees who undermine its chance for success.

Tie atrophy

If a limb is not used it will atrophy. Its sensitivity and functionality become severely degraded.

Companies have similar problems where their willingness and ability to serve external relations are limited, causing tie atrophy. Tie atrophy is characterized by insufficient and ineffective exploitation of external relationships that leads to the limited and irregular flow of resources and information.

Organizational relationships weaken if not properly utilized. Their capacities and functionality become limited. Companies become unable to attract and serve customers which will end with a total inability to develop fruitful ties and secure the smooth flow of resources. Key customers and partners leave, and their resources and information are no longer available.

One of my old friends, a Business Development Director of a large grocery distributor once said to me: "We were focused on big contracts, ignoring small buyers. Things changed and we realized that we lost the ability to work with smaller companies which is frightening. We are losing daily. I'm not sure we will survive this year unless we retrain a sales team to new conditions very quickly. However, small shops are not willing to work with us now. This is a bigger problem."

If a company has lost a part of its external relations, then it means that it has lost the relevant part of the market. It is doubtful the organization can survive relying on random relationships with customers and trimmed cash flow. Whilst ignoring their own important functions and constant exchange with customers and partners, a business with tie atrophy must be prepared to be ignored by others in return, which is very costly for anyone. In simple terms tie atrophy ruins the whole idea of a customer-centered business.

Tie atrophy comes from underperforming customer-facing staff. In most cases they show low competence in serving customers and require advanced training.

Misleading instructions from incompetent leaders often add more weight to this problem, as in the case of the distribution company where my friend works. Such leaders should be removed.

Incoordination syndrome

Start-ups and rapidly growing companies commonly face similar problems with assigning roles and ineffective internal communication, and so don't fully control functions of effectiveness and resource utilization. Large companies face similar issues when middle managers abuse their power. In other words, poorly managed companies, and particularly those with negative corporate culture, face a life-threatening disease – incoordination syndrome.

This disease can lead to a complete loss of internal stability. Incoordination syndrome causes a sharp increase in governance costs. The company becomes too expensive to operate.

This problem directly affects organizational metabolism, i.e., simultaneous performance of all functions and departments. Incoordination syndrome is the result of poor and inappropriate organizational design and structural composition, where the roles are not clearly defined, execution of duties is poorly controlled, performance is measured only within the frames of a single department or unit, and corporate culture is negative and demotivating.

Such a diagnosis reveals a company that has become scarcely controlled and almost unmanageable, making it an easy target for competitors and vulnerable to hijacking. Incoordination syndrome also provides fertile soil for internal corruption which has ruined many companies.

Treatment of this disease demands a serious revision of management structure as it is responsible for the execution of all tasks while corporate culture demands even more serious attention as it is responsible for leveraging inconsistencies in formal and informal internal relations.

Muteness

Muteness is associated with an inability or limited ability to talk and articulate messages clearly. However, people with such a problem can use gestures to convey their thoughts and feelings. It is not a death risk unless it is a sign of a fatal neurological disease like Lou Gehrig's disease (Amyotrophic lateral sclerosis) which causes the death of neurons and resulting difficulties in speaking and breathing.

Muteness is a deadly disease for any company. The business loses its ability to serve and exploit its external ties effectively. It still makes noise but is not able to communicate clearly with stakeholders and customers in particular. Modern customers are not willing to support such a business. If the signals transmitted externally are vague, they don't attract the attention of customers with other choices.

Ineffective communication costs a fortune. I estimate that meaningless meetings and vague messages cost a devastating loss of $2 million to $5 million each year to a medium size company, and many times more for large companies. Small businesses simply can't afford to waste any time at all.

Muteness reflects an internal inability to read and understand market requirements and ineffectiveness of every function designed to interface with the market. More and more energy and resources are wasted on communication without the desired results.

Cross syndrome

Let's imagine a company whose posture is hunched like someone with advanced Parkinson's. In corporate terms, this is cross syndrome, which relates to cases of the dominance of one function over others without an appropriate reason. This problem undermines the balanced structural composition that was originally established to achieve the desired effectiveness.

Cross syndrome results in the malfunctioning of one department and unrewarding hyperactivity in other departments. In practice, poor managers are preoccupied with their importance, high workload, and blaming colleagues from other departments for their own poor performance. They treat it as a game, but the consequences for the business are extremely serious.

A company affected with this disease faces harsh functional pitfalls, low overall performance, and insufficient organizational endurance. The company's business model becomes ineffective as it acts not as one whole body but a set of separated and unfriendly units. The company can't resist environmental challenges anymore.

One of my clients, the building materials producer, experienced this problem. The marketing department was doing practically nothing while doing an excellent job of appearing busy. However, their results were next to nothing. The Head of the Department and his team were very effective at blaming sales and production departments. The workload of these departments increased due to the execution of unrelated tasks. In fact, three departments were underperforming – the marketing department because of poor work, sales and production departments which were constantly blamed appeared exhausted and underperforming while wasting a lot of time correcting the mistakes of others. Treatment of cross syndrome, in this case, allowed the company to increase the turnover by 13% or almost $11 million in real money.

Cross syndrome can be caused by poor leaders being in charge of functional departments. Initially, they turn a blind eye to the problem and come to allow such behavior.

Stiffness

Old-fashioned governance routines and practices resist innovation. Large companies are like big ships moving in a predefined direction. They rely on robust systems and settled processes and are not prepared for serious innovation. They feel comfortable as they are. They create some sort of comfort and stability while every innovation demands unwelcome change.

Internal systems that were set long ago cause a painful side effect – stiffness. Traditionally, this pathology is associated with old organizations.

While often considered an age-related problem, stiffness can be diagnosed in companies of any age with the negative culture in which excessive formalities, complicated and conflicting rules, and policies limit corporate flexibility, preparedness to change, and capacity to adapt. Stiffness does not allow the company to react to market dynamics.

Stiffness is a purely psychological problem related to a certain type of decision-making in which leaders emphasize their power over people. It restricts natural development, quickly turning into a physical problem. Stiffness restricts business from progressing along with the market.

Treating stiffness is not so much a matter of restructuring or reorganization. Stiffness demands the necessary changes to be made in approach and policy, and quality of leadership.

General diseases

There are a number of problems and diseases that can be diagnosed in companies of all types, affecting their general ability to conduct business effectively. The most common are resource blindness, weather sensitivity, and dystrophy.

Resource blindness

"It doesn't matter how many resources you have if you don't know how to use them, they will never be enough." I don't know who the author of this brilliant quote is, but I salute him or her for the perfect description of a very peculiar corporate disease – resource blindness.

Unfortunately, leaders and managers often fail to recognize the spectrum of resources critical for their business. A specific organizational diet that allows a company to perform at its best remains unclear for leaders suffering from resource blindness. Critically important resources are undervalued, and secondary ones are praised. As a result, time, funds, and effort are wasted on unimportant things costing millions.

For instance, I faced a case of resource blindness in a large clinic in Moscow. The management was mainly concerned about sales training and purchasing of fancy equipment which wasn't properly used while ignoring the development of expertise of its own medical consultants as a core asset. This problem cost the clinic a few years of organic growth before being recognized and treated.

It may sound strange for twenty-first-century businesses where a high percentage of managers with advanced business degrees have the acute need for clear resource classification training, but it is necessary. Also, a company will perform much better if employees are clearly aware of what resources must be developed and how to add value to them.

Weather sensitivity

The demand for a wide range of products and services can be affected by weather or season. This can be seen in the fluctuations in the consumption of ice cream or fresh meat, open-air events like sports and entertainment, farming, fishing, or travel.

The majority of businesses are weather sensitive, and their activities can be affected by hot, cold, or windy weather. Weather sensitivity is related to the change in demand caused by consumers' behavior in different weather conditions.

No one can control the weather but being prepared for slow seasons is not something extraordinary, like having other products in the portfolio or enacting cost reduction programs. This problem is fairly common, and the majority of organizations have policies to deal with it. However, it is still entertaining to hear that, for instance, the fact it was snowing in winter was a surprise for a northern town's city council.

Dystrophy

Whether a business is prepared and capable of satisfying sudden exceptionally high demand or not defines its prospects for getting into higher value markets. For instance, some companies and particularly start-ups dream about global dominance but often cannot handle a massive influx of customers and will collapse overnight.

This problem is attributed to organizational dystrophy. Dystrophy shows the constant lack of resources and capacities to fulfill its promises to the market. This disease is accompanied by the inefficiency of processes, limited access to resources, regular underfinancing, and policies and practices that artificially limit a company's capabilities in serving the demand. It simply restricts growth and forces a company to let excellent opportunities pass by.

Dystrophy shows that processes and functions are weak and have limited flexibility. When the dystrophy occurs in start-ups or young companies, we tend to blame underfinancing on undefined processes and trial periods. However, more dangerous cases can be observed in mature companies where the dystrophy comes as a result of incompetent managerial decisions. Management provokes the dystrophy by concentrating on a limited number of performance indicators and thus, show a faulty understanding of the richness and complexity of the company and its potentials.

Imagine a company saying to customers – "we can't solve your problems as we are busy solving our own." In fact, this happens far too often.

Also, functional dystrophy must be mentioned as well. It comes as a result of inappropriate role distribution between functions, irrelevant structural dependencies, and poor planning. A functional department not designed for high performance receives little attention and care, does not develop along with the rest of the business and eventually gets dystrophic and unproductive. It does not add value to the overall strategic goal. I have seen this practice, particularly in underperforming HR departments.

Organizational dystrophy is more typical for start-ups and small-sized companies, whereas functional dystrophy can be diagnosed in businesses of all sizes.

Conclusion

Organizational health is the responsibility of all leaders. This chapter discussed only common problems and diseases where the leaders' work is to observe his businesses and recognize typical problems and diseases and develop remedies against them. Successful businesses face the same or maybe even greater problems, but they are masterful in solving them effectively.

ORGANIZATIONAL HEALTH IS THE RESPONSIBILITY OF all LEADERS

All businesses are purely pragmatic in the sense of their existence, goals, and logic of external and internal processes. They are built to explore market potentials and serve customers while overcoming problems that are an unavoidable part of human and business life. Effective exploitation of organizational capacities is only possible if a company is treated as a whole and not as fragmented parts.

Practical tips

- Don't multiply problems or try to solve them all at once. Go simply by solving the clearest one in a structured way and then move to the next.

- A leader's job is to direct people in problem-solving. Leaders are accountable for gaps in performance and, by definition, they are the chief problem solvers.

- A company doesn't create problems itself. Problems are the result of poor leadership and the negative culture created by it.

- Don't wait for the problems to disappear on their own. Problems must be treated quickly. Otherwise, they will grow into sinister trends if untreated.

- The earlier a problem is diagnosed, the less effort the treatment will demand.

- Problem-solving actions are based on accepting reality, mental flexibility, preparedness for change, and artful execution of assigned duties. If needed, asking other people for help is often a necessity which allows faster problem solving. Actions, and not words, are what count when dealing with problems. Words without action will only make it worse.

- The ability to make balanced decisions comes from the ability to listen to the whole body of an organization without neglecting small details, whilst bearing in mind the core goal of serving customers. This demands a good understanding of the organization's living nature and knowledge of how to exploit its capacity in the most effective way.

- Overall effectiveness is the result of activities of all departments working together to add value. A problem in one function ripples out, echoing in the capacities of other departments.

- Problems and diseases tend to return if not treated properly and the lessons weren't learned. They just hide deeper in processes and routines, reappearing in different mutated forms again and again.

Chapter Eleven

THIRTY LESSONS I LEARNED ABOUT LEADERSHIP

Leadership is a lifelong journey through different experiences every day. Every situation, every experience, every lesson learned sheds more light on this enormously demanding duty.

This chapter offers thirty lessons as a reflection of my leadership experience. I am not claiming that all my experience is unique but just as important as experience is what we learn from it. Some lessons were immediate while the value of some I realized only with time. Some I learned from others and still others came at a hefty price.

1. Don't rush to call yourself a leader. Learn how to change your own self first and how to serve people. No leader can make a difference for people without being true to his self.

Learn about people and their needs and apply this knowledge daily by helping people. Learn how to make small steps while dreaming big.

2. True leaders must be with people, not just near them. Those who only monitor people tend to

think – "Are they doing well? If yes, then I am a good leader." This is wrong. Are you giving input to the team? Are you present when things are going well or only if things go poorly? If there is no actual input into the team, then the leader is just a user of people's energy, an energy vampire. How much effort and energy the leader puts into the work defines the actual role and status of the leader.

3. Be a coach and receptive learner at the same time. This is the best combination. On one hand, you help people to grow by sharing your expertise. Knowledge and passion must be shared otherwise it will die from lack of use. Their viability will expire with time if not shared, much like food going bad. Don't hold your knowledge close to your chest. Share as much as you can with people. In turn, as people know more, they will achieve greater heights.

On the other hand, not learning from people is equal to ignoring them. Also, having experts on the team from whom the leader and the entire team can learn and benefit is a true gift. Life provides opportunities to learn from the many different people and experiences we encounter. To get the most from such opportunities, one must be willing to listen and give your full attention to others.

4. Appreciate everything that is given to you. Life gives something good to a leader not for personal use but to share with others. Keep gifting

people with what you have. Sharing demonstrates appreciation for the chance to be a leader to the people for working with you. Appreciation also allows space for new capacities needed for new achievements. Otherwise, you will get nothing next time if you don't value what you have.

5.   Leadership is not a dictatorship. No leader should be corrupted by his power. All that power and influence should be used to serve people. They will pay threefold back with respect, support, and loyalty. Make your leadership worth following. Be an example, not just king of the mountain in a kid's game. Leadership means being very human and working for others.

6.   The leader develops people. Many need help exploring their potential. At the same time, human desires are not always expressed directly. In this sense, helping people explore themselves and grow is a great and rewarding privilege. They will appreciate a leader who helps them flourish by focusing on their strengths. People will be more open to coaching and less defensive.

7.   Leadership is an art. Being artful in leadership means seeing the beauty in people, in the diversity of their feelings and desires, and finding unique solutions for every demand. Learn about art, nature, and other things which would nourish your creativity and a keen eye for beauty. How can one create something beautiful for people if one can't

see beauty in everyday things like smiles or the change of seasons?

A grand master and a street artist may use the same canvas and same oil paint, but one makes a masterpiece and the other makes kitsch. The difference is in the ability to see beauty and bring it to others. Business needs more masterpieces as markets are packed with low-value reproductions.

8. Lifelong learner and leader are synonymous. Learning allows one to explore something new, seeing new perspectives every time, and finding how to get them working for people. What a leader brings to the table tomorrow comes from what has been learned yesterday and today. If nothing new has been learned, then there is nothing new to be offered.

9. A modern leader is a servant. Employees and customers are personal clients of the leader. Their success and satisfaction is a leader's biggest concern. The leader takes the most responsibility in the room for the company, employees, culture, and customer satisfaction. Therefore, the leader is rewarded based on what difference he or she has made for people to secure their professional and personal growth. If there is nothing to report, then the leader should be removed.

10. Leaders inspire trust in others. When people trust a leader, they trust each other easier and collaborate more effectively. If employees don't trust leaders, then they only trust each other.

11.   The leader is an ambassador within his organization and beyond, representing the interests and desires of employees and customers. The duty is to defend employees and customers against mistakes, against unfair blame, and against biases and doubts. People will defend a leader if they are defended by him.

12.   A leader's wisdom and humility go hand in hand. Being humble makes it easy to treat others sincerely, with kindness and respect no matter who they are. Humility helps to strengthen connections between leaders and employees. Humble leaders never put themselves above others and gain true supporters at all levels. Snobby leaders have only a few flunkeys next to them busy with precooked praises. They barely see people at all.

13.   An effective leader must have the means of honest self-reflection and growth – a mentor, coach, or a critical friend, at least. Self-reflection is not enough as the subjective leads to people rationalizing mistakes rather than learning from them. The battle against one's own weakness will be lost because of this. A good mentor helps one to learn about himself or herself and others while offering suggestions for improvement. A mentor's experience doubles or even triples a mentee's experience, defining personal and professional growth.

14.   Freedom of thoughts comes from reflection. From another perspective, sincere reflection allows

actual personal growth and helps one prepare for new challenges. In reality, one could go days and weeks in a row without a minute for reflection. Create opportunities to relax and reflect.

15. Wise leaders take present success as a step to future achievements. They recharge, learn the new lay of the land, and get ready to work hard again. Leadership is a never-ending journey where every single mile is full of new tests and trials. You must consciously allow for the re-examination of your approach frequently to be successful in the future.

16. The support of someone strong inspires and gives extra strength to those who are weaker. Encouraging people means nourishing their minds and injecting their soul and body with energy for action. For many, a leader's encouragement is equal to drinking "living water," reviving them for new challenges. People will always appreciate this kind of support.

17. A leader must be a rock and ensure the vision of the prospective future is much greater than any problems. Confidence in inevitable success brings calmness and effectiveness in achieving goals. If a leader is not confident in what he or she is doing, then employees will be even less so. If a leader is confident and calm, employees are calm and confident as well.

18. A leader's personal courage is important, but the team's courage is superior in securing success. A leader can't move further than the team. The inspired team doesn't need pushing or pulling but only a nudge in the right direction. An ability to inspire is worth a fortune.

19. The level or grade of leadership is defined by the sustainability of decisions one makes. High level leadership reflects decisions with broader impact, with greater meaning for all involved. Low-level leadership is characterized by more patterned decisions that only allow random or marginal success which don't move the company forward.

20. A thoughtful leader always appreciates diversity. Every role and duty is important. Gender diversity offers different mental and emotional qualities of men and women in the team. People of different ages with different experiences, qualities, and talents complement each other and enrich the overall team's capacity.

21. Real leaders over-deliver on promises and work hard to achieve a shared vision. They calculate the potentials, the risks, and the effort needed. Real leaders know well that they will be judged against actual deeds and fulfilled promises. Unfulfilled promises work against them and people who counted on them will leave. Promising too much is for incompetent leaders.

22. There is no leader without self-discipline. Self-discipline means establishing an authority over one's own habits, routines, and priorities, and not being under their control. The leader is a model of self-discipline and purposefulness with hands always directed to the task at hand. The leader is always busy doing something for tomorrow without being told what to do and how to do it. Self-discipline is a mandatory resource for every leader. Otherwise, how can he tell people what to do if he can't control himself?

23. The leader is a source of specific energy which influences and drives people. This is the energy of inspiration and acting. It doesn't put the leader above all, but it defines the place inside the team as a source and distributor of this energy which allows the shared vision to take root and prosper.

24. Leaders invest in people's growth. They invest their effort and knowledge; they believe in people and shape them for the future. By doing so, the leader becomes better and more needed. Whether one is investing or devoting one's self to employees or not defines the difference between the leader and corporate status chaser.

25. Culture reflects leadership. Leaders define and maintain the culture and teach employees how to take care of it. Competencies and growth of employees depend on what culture the leader cultivates – positive or negative. Thus, leaders must

be fair, looking at culture as a mirror which reflects how they work successfully with people.

26. The leader should clearly know own leadership capacity. Leadership assumes certain capacities depending on the size and complexity of the managed organization. Think of the pilots confirming their capacity to fly different aircraft. They must obtain a different type of license for different kinds of aircraft, from a sports pilot license to an airline transport pilot license.

If one tries to pilot out of his capacity it will lead to disaster. Setting a bar low doesn't help anyone to win the future.

27. The leader must be persistent like Don Quixote in chasing his vision, protecting it, in seeing what others don't see. Persistence allows us to run long distances and help others to win as well, regardless of how far the goal is set. For the persistent, upcoming uncertainties only inspire active thinking to find new methods and approaches. However, in modern terms, persistence must be for the sake of the whole team and not one's own ego.

28. The leader is a doer with vision. There are two other practices that can poison the future, having vision without doing or doing without vision. They undermine the core meaning of leadership. Such leaders fail to stimulate loyalty, or effort, or even simple sympathy. No one is willing to sweat

in purposeless activities or wait without reason for a miracle to happen.

29. Winners breed winners. It is a leader's duty to help people to feel like winners even in small achievements, to convince them of their ability to succeed despite past failure. This will help them to be prepared for the greater wins. Let your employees feel the awesome sensation of success in their guts and let them feel like an important part of that success. People trained to win will win. People trained to fail will fail.

30. The leader is an expert in catching momentum. Never underestimate but praise your people's capabilities and achievements. Use the momentum of what you have at hand by praising your employees' capabilities and achievements and use it to strengthen the link between the company and customers. Use this momentum to win people's hearts.

To conclude this chapter, I want to stress that leaders are masters of simplicity who bring order by conquering chaos in people's minds and actions, bring people together, and building confidence for the future. Thus, great leaders are always in demand as people need them and their unique qualities to complement and develop theirs.

Part Four

LEADEROLOGY

We are facing a massive shortage of effective leaders, and the demand is only growing. Modern management desperately needs a systematic and robust understanding of leadership. We stand on the brink of a great unknown. Reliance on the personal experience of even very successful leaders is not sufficient anymore. What was okay and even good just ten years ago is not sufficient anymore, it can even cause harm.

While talking about a revolution in management caused by the realities of the Knowledge Era and the Digital Era, we need to think about who will lead this revolution and who will take care of business after. We need to stimulate the evolution of management thinking and acting in terms of people's growth and customer's satisfaction.

The Knowledge Era has clearly demonstrated that we can't progress further without developing leadership capabilities on a global scale. Whether in public, private, or political organizations, leadership is responsible for the maintenance and functioning of effective businesses as systems of satisfying customers.

A leader's serendipity in finding successful strategies and effective solutions and approaches depend on a well-homogenized mixture of vision, competencies, intuition, luck, knowledge, focus, and concern of others. Here we should think of leaderology, a new but necessary term.

Leaderology, is it science or art? Leaderology is about helping people to discover their hidden leadership qualities and learning to face the necessity to change on a systematic basis.

Chapter Twelve

LEADEROLOGY

I nearly caused a heart attack in a number of CEOs and owners of large and medium companies from different countries with one seemingly simple question – How easy is it to find decent leaders for different top and senior positions for your business?

Their responses were surprisingly similar – "Don't rub salt in the wound," "This is a pain," "I wish I knew the answer." As a CEO of a medium but fast-growing software company said to me – "Finding a leader, not just manager… is like looking for a unicorn."

If we look at this issue from the viewpoint of the next generation of leaders the situation is much the same as that faced by current CEOs. Those who are still learning about business and leadership are already infused with the false belief that the only real leaders are those few who already run huge corporations, fly private jets, and go to meetings in helicopters.

Overall, the problem is that a decent leader is often considered to be a superman, a miracle worker infallibly leading people from success to success.

We seem more prepared to believe leadership is really a mysterious power given to a few rather than the result of experience and hard work.

The father of modern management, Peter Drucker (2009, p. 26) stated years ago that "No institution can possibly survive if it needs geniuses or supermen to manage it. It must be organized in such a way as to be able to get along under a leadership composed of average human beings."

We are still hesitant to stop trying to create leaders by using approaches and techniques from the Industrial Era. We fail to consider that such a decades' old approach fails in the new and radically demanding conditions of the Digital Age. Reliance on a few prominently gifted leaders is not enough anymore.

At the same, new emerging contextual factors make leadership as a critical function even more complex and demanding than ever before - changes in people management, technologies, the growing importance of diversity and inclusion, shifts in national cultures, and many more. We are well into a new phase of business evolution, a fact businesspeople ignore or struggle to accept.

The demand for leaders capable of growing people and creating appropriate conditions for growth shows that competent leadership becomes more important than anything else in terms of driving businesses for success.

We urgently need to break out of the old paradigm of leadership and develop something new and relevant to the realities of the Digital Era. It is a choice between life and death for our businesses.

A leader is defined by the people who stand with him

A leader is not defined as single person with all the power and responsibility. Rather, he is part of a team, a team he encourages and inspires. He faces challenges and achieves success with the team. The leader learns from his team and them from him. To be a leader, one must be accepted as such by his employees.

In this sense, leadership is a system of collaboration and interdependency between leaders and employees that allows them to achieve the organization's goals while emphasizing authenticity and individual growth.

It is critically important that leaders execute their duties well, but what is more important is how those duties affect the leaders. The duties and stresses of leadership can change a person, for good or ill.

If a personality is weak, then those duties will break down that personality very quickly, turning him into someone full of fear and envy. For those mediocre leaders, life becomes a mass of uncertainty. They rely on fear, intimidation, and processes as their main leadership instruments. Ignorance of hard work and effort in learning and everyday growth are their main attributes.

If a leader has a strong personality, the duties of leadership will make that person even stronger. Such leaders grow in confidence and skill from one task to the next, thriving on the challenges presented.

Good leaders grow together with their people and not at their expense. They assume responsibility for the growth and achievements and failures of the people under them. Strong leaders believe in and praise hard work, training, and preparation over mere expectations.

GOOD LEADERS GROW TOGETHER with their People and not at their expense

They all have a strong will to make a difference for people, devoting themselves to life-long self-improvement to better fulfill this responsibility. That will help them to fight fears, self-doubts, and thousands of "no's" from naysayers. They learn to be prepared for many different possible scenarios. As an ancient Greek poet, Archilochus said in 650 BC. "We don't rise to the level of our expectations; we fall to the level of our training."

At the same time, we can say that a craving for learning is associated with natural curiosity, driving one to learn more in different areas, allowing out-of-the-box thinking in various situations. While reading the same book different people learn different lessons and are inspired in unique ways. Good leaders gain multiple lessons and impressions and act on the inspiration that follows.

Business involves discovery and leaders must be explorers of new and effective business solutions. This requires them to be bolder than their conservative and cautious predecessors. They face new and difficult to predict cases daily. These new problems will require new solutions, solutions that will have to come from adaptable and decisive thinkers.

Flexibility and a high level of adaptability allow leaders to analyze information from multiple perspectives using it in the best ways to ensure company, employee, and personal growth. This is not an exact science. Rather, it should be treated like an art. These are few hard and fast rules but many guidelines, guidelines that allow for a great deal of freedom.

From leadership to leaderology

If leadership is so important for the existence and success of all organizations, then we desperately need a new system for leading businesses. Leaderology is a system of systematic knowledge, competencies, and skills that allow an effective aligning of the organization, culture, and the most appropriate modes of leadership to serve customers effectively. It is a response to the growing complexity of duties and tasks in the Digital Era.

In other words, success in business should have a code that defines its feasibility. The aim of leaderology is to find these codes of success for different businesses.

Aligning business as an effective composition of the company, culture, and leadership is creating harmony between the interrelation of a real entity (company), love and care of employees and customers (culture), and vision (leadership).

How do these three elements complement each other to satisfy customer demand? A company is a real entity with boundaries within which employees act. These boundaries are not physical. Whatever employees act out in their imagination, thinking about their duties while not in the office, or representing the company formally and informally in different situation, these are the borders within which we fulfill our roles and duties towards company, colleagues, and customers.

A company exists to the extent it allows a positive culture to flourish and facilitate common wisdom, love, and care. Culture as love and care transforms an organization from a mere place of work to a place where people can become better than they are. People inside and outside the organization will be affected by this.

Take these three elements separately and they will fall apart. Masterfully aligning the company, its culture, and specific leadership traits can be considered as the first element of the code of business success.

The second part of that code lies in the ability of leaders to add vision, strength, value, and focus to every element of business to satisfy customers while securing their people's growth and sustainable development of their organizations. Success in business is based on a simple approach – understand customer demand, form your vision, assess your resources, and bring them together.

Practical tips

- A genuine leader is not one who is capable of everything but excellent in empowering people and giving them a chance to grow. Such a leader helps to roll out a red carpet for people and to become leaders themselves. Help people to take their own journey into a successful future by helping them to become more competent and competitive, supporting them with your own experience.

- Bad leaders build barriers for people. Strong leaders build barriers to problems, accidents, and stagnation. We have more than enough mediocre or bad leaders. We need strong leaders for real progress and to make a positive difference in people's lives.

- Too much thinking about the future without vision and focus on people while skipping today's duties often blinds leaders to the present. A strong present lays a solid path into the future. We often fail to appreciate what we have now.

- Many leaders don't fight, giving up far too quickly. They worry too much about themselves and not enough about reaching their goals and so fail to inspire.

Chapter Thirteen

FACING THE FUTURE, RISING HIGH

*"The Future belongs to those
that can hear it coming!"*
—David Bowie

Future is the Realm of Positivity. The prospects we can foresee are genuine and promising in terms of human growth and developing new possibilities for all. Even the mere word "future" has an effect. It can thrill, excite, energize, and disturb.

Every morning we wake up to a new reality – new thoughts, emotions, impressions, challenges, and decisions. We look forward to meeting new people and discovering something new. Depending on how positively we meet a new sunrise, the day will be positive as well. The same happens for the future. If we are positive in our expectations of the future, we are more likely to build a positive reality.

There is no bad weather, but you can dress badly for the weather. The same is true about the future, it is a matter of how we prepare for it. Those who are prepared become active participants in that future and enjoy the fruits of that preparation. Those who are not prepared become cynical neurotics harming themselves with their glass-half-empty attitude.

Making new mistakes in the new future is normal. What is not normal is to take old mistakes into the future. In other words, don't use old tattered sails to navigate what is to come.

What should be considered and what kind of changes should businesses be prepared for? The motto of modern business should be *cura customer* (latin - care of customer). This reflects the ever-growing effort and responsibility of businesses to satisfy customers. There is no place or time for cheap talk or meaningless shouting across a marketplace which becomes ineffective and even annoying. Focus on connecting with people now and in the future.

An old wise man was asked – "why are people shouting at each other?" He responded – "At this moment their hearts are standing too far from each other even though they are standing in front of each other."

The rise of the digital world presents opportunities that few could dream of just a generation ago. Connecting hearts and minds is the ultimate goal of digitalization, helping people to develop together as one progressive force. Digitalization helps us to explore new dimensions in our business and personal lives. It will ultimately change the way we act and think.

An old English proverb says, "You can lead a horse to water, but you can't make it drink." We have an enormous opportunity to be connected thanks to digitalization, and it would be a waste not to use it. Some forward-thinking businesses are already enjoying this momentum, allowing them to get closer to customers, others are still resisting and will be forced to use it or disappear completely.

Let's use these opportunities that digitalization offers us to connect. This demands sophisticated skills and competencies, the foremost being the managing of emotions. For this, a business should first know itself, making it much easier to understand customers and built strong ties with them.

From leadership to leaderology

The future can't be met with backward-thinking and old leadership methods that are no longer effective. Leaders need to become advocates of continuous development. The leader's duty is to open a door into the future for people and explain how things should be considered and managed in that new reality.

The LEADER'S DUTY is to OPEN A DOOR into THE FUTURE...

This demands more knowledge, advanced competencies, and systematic thinking. Those moving first and exploring new realities for others should be armed with more knowledge, advanced competencies, and long-term thinking.

We are moving from leadership as a function to leaderology as a system of leading and making a difference for people. Leaders face more responsibilities and much higher expectations in terms of the execution of their roles. The leader's responsibilities are expanding enormously, demanding much stronger competencies and skills than before. Everyday learning and continuous improvement need to be the norm.

The modern leader needs to combine meticulous planning with flexibility. Combining these attributes is necessary in an ever-changing and hyper-competitive market. The wrong decisions and actions can lead to the whole organization losing sight of customer needs as well as quality, harming the long-term sustainability of the organization. Making the right decisions means thinking of more than the company. It means considering the values and needs of customers and employees as well.

A leader's role is manifold, being change ambassadors for employees and educators and inspirers for customers. In this sense, the leader being a mentor, coach, and authority is critically important to consistently add value to people.

Businesses should become more and more accountable for their actions. There is no place for the old-style approach where the leader makes decisions without input from employees. Decisions should be based on the needs of employees and well as those of the organization.

Leaders are influencers and disruptors whose job is not to motivate people only for a short time but inspire them for long-term action. To do this, the leader must have a deep commitment to the organization's goals.

Culture

It is necessary to reimagine the role of culture as one of the most important elements of management, and one of the main functions of leadership. Advanced qualities and competencies of people must be developed and mobilized if the company aims to remain competitive. Culture offers the most versatile instruments in growing and nurturing talents which must be consistently and artfully used.

Productive culture means effective communication. A workplace becomes a place of interaction and collaboration between employees and customers, with all necessary options and gadgets securing the highest quality of transferring meaning and information between people.

The entire team is responsible for the mutual growth and engagement of every member. This is a matter of productive interdependency and advanced engagement for the sake of customer and employee satisfaction.

Modern organization is not a mere assortment of random ideas but a multidimensional and multi-view approach to solving customers' problems. Success directly depends on how much value is delivered to the customer.

Thanks to the modern understanding of culture, businesses have learned the enormous power of diversity at the workplace. For instance, we have learned the indispensable role of women and their power which bring incredible advantages and fresh opportunities. We have only scratched the surface here, much still need to be done in this direction.

Culture is alive and dynamic in its nature. This is a living system which prospers if treated with full attention at every stage of development. It must be attuned to people if we want to release its full force.

Organization

A modern company should be built and managed precisely to its purpose and nature.

Otherwise, customers have difficulty finding it in the overcrowded marketplace while in turn, the company has tremendous difficulty in recognizing and satisfying customer needs. Every little problem puts distance between the business and its customers. Thus, managers' competencies in diagnosing problems and treating them effectively are vitally important for businesses concerned with long life and success.

Three critical points of future organizations arise in this sense. Firstly, a company should enhance its nature while adapting and using new technologies such as AI (Artificial Intelligence), blockchain, and others, focusing how they can best be used to serve others. A living organization has unlimited potential for growth and development where mechanical ones have strict limits for development. In any case, nothing can replace human interaction. Otherwise, it is like sending a robot to a date and asking it to describe the first kiss or asking a machine after a of day fishing about the adrenaline rush of hooking a strong fish. Collaboration and interaction in an organization is both natural and necessary.

Secondly, being lean and focused is essential to an effective company. Excessive and inefficient functions built into processes is not a sign of wealth but of decadence. Such companies become heavy, slow, and non-productive, and fall hard. We should expect a swift and massive fall of those strong businesses if they can't cope with the requirements of the digital age. The requirements of the Digital

Era act like fine filters on how organizations should be purposed and configured.

Thirdly, products and services must be compliant to the modern requirements dictated by the Digital Era. Does your company produce a digital adaptive or digital friendly product or service? This is the modern reality and is necessary for progression to the next level of development. Future success will rely heavily on recognizing opportunities and potentials offered by digitalization.

Getting out of your comfort zone

The Digital Era demands going out of our comfort zone. What does this mean in the present context? This is the accustomed and habitual paradigm of thinking and acting; something that doesn't demand much effort and change.

Getting out of a comfort zone demands risk-taking, effort, learning, and vision in terms of why an unfamiliar action should be done. Doing so might exact a cost for breaking out of a mental and psychological cage. Enhancing the future means being willing to enter a new state of mind.

Also, we should consider that the resistance of naysayers will be tougher than ever. They are chronically dependent on stillness in their lives and not prepared for such changes. Naysayers are those who want to pay neither with effort nor with forward thinking. They don't see what can be gained and are afraid to lose a familiar routine. They are afraid they will be forced to do something unusual in the future.

At the same time, the visionaries of the future must be grateful to them for their critiques and help in find even better solutions.

Rising high

The more we explore about business, the clearer we see its contours, and the more of it we can use. We are drawing a new map of the business world. The twenty-first century is a time for sustainable development demanding continuous improvement, exploring new areas of human demands, and discovering new markets and industries.

We improve by opening minds and hearts while supporting others. By doing so, we not only lift ourselves but future generations as well. Every business is responsible for the future of coming generations.

Upcoming generations will learn from us. We are obliged to build a solid platform for further progress. We must inject them with a spirit of exploration, care for people, and a craving for learning. Our job is to show them that falling and rising is normal and the best way to grow. They should inherit a keen eye for opportunities, creating potentials, and continuous value-creation. The stronger platform we build for them, the further they will reach.

Thank you for reading this book. The last thing I want to say on these pages - Smile, as you know how to build a strong successful business. Smile, as you are fully capable of it. Smile, as you have everything at hand. Smile, as you are about to explore something new and make a difference for the people right now and the years ahead.

Acknowledgements

Writing a book is a long journey which can't be completed without support of those who believe in you. Thanks for the incredible support of my loving wife, Zagidat, for sharing the pressure during this journey.

I am very grateful to Eric Postma for his valuable editorial suggestions and comments, and overall support.

Special praises to Dr. Carmel de Nahlik for her insightful comments and sharp ideas.

I would also like to thank all my respondents for sharing their experiences, invaluable insights, supporting this project, and helping to explore new areas of discussion.

References

Archilochus. Top 12 Quotes by Archilochus. https://www.azquotes.com/author/20957-Archilochus

AnyGood? 2018. Trust in Recruitment. http://trustinrecruitment.com/wp-content/uploads/TrustInRec_Insights.pdf

Böckerman, Petri, and Ilmakunnas, Pekka. 2012. The Job Satisfaction-Productivity Nexus: A Study Using Matched Survey and Register Data, *Industrial & Labor Relations Review*, Volume 65, Number 2, p. 244-263

Coelho, Paulo. 2006. *The Zahir: A Novel of Obsession*. Harper Perennial.

Gallup Employee Engagement Report. 2018. https://www.gallup.com/topic/employee_engagement.aspx

Goldsmith, Marshall. 2013. *What got you here, won't get you there*. USA. Profile Books Ltd.

Daskal, Lolly. 2017. *The Leadership Gap: What Gets Between You and Your Greatness*. Portfolio

Drucker, Peter F. 2009. *Concept of the Corporation*.

Transaction Publishers

Drucker, Peter. F. 1973. *Management: Tasks, Responsibilities, Practices*. E.P. Ed. New York. Truman Talley Books.

Etzioni, Amitai. 1964. *Modern Organizations*. USA. Prentice-Hall.

Gogh, Vincent van. 1937. *Dear Theo: An Autobiography of Vincent Van Gogh*. http://www. nsrider.com/quotes/life.htm

Konovalov, Oleg. 2016. *Organisational Anatomy: A Manager's Guide To A Healthy Organisation*. Newcastle, UK. Cambridge Scholars Publishing. Newcastle, UK

Konovalov, Oleg. 2018. *Corporate Superpower: Cultivating A Winning Culture For Your Business*. USA. WildBlue Press.

Lyons, Martyn. 1994. *Napoleon Bonaparte and the Legacy of the French Revolution*. New York: St. Martin's Press.

Porsche   Ferry   https://www.porsche.com/ international/aboutporsche/70-years/history/

Shaw, George Bernard. 2018. *Man and Superman*. Otbebook Publishing

UK Parliament Report. 2019. Small Businesses and Productivity. Part 6. Late Payments, Retentions and Government Procurement. https://publications.parliament.uk/pa/cm201719/cmselect/cmbeis/807/80709.htm#footnote-112

World Economic Forum. 2018. The Digital Enterprise: Moving from experimentation to transformation. https://www.weforum.org/ reports/the-digital-enterpise-moving-from-experimentation-to-transformation

Chapter One

Live, Immaterial, and Functional

Since the time of Cicero, people have tended to take the phenomenon of culture for granted, often assuming that it is synonymous with organizational culture. However, a more specialized understanding of organizational culture began to coalesce some decades ago. In fact, it was first described as a group climate by Lewin, Lippitt, and White in 1939. Subsequently, in the mid-seventies, organizational norms, roles, and values were viewed in terms of the social psychology of organizations, although, at that stage, it was not explicitly stated as organizational climate or culture. Since then, a large number of definitions have appeared, serving to confirm the complex nature of this incorporeal being. However, we are still exploring this elephant in a dark room.

Culture does not exist in an isolated and purified environment without the presence of other people. Culture is a complex phenomenon, deeply interpenetrating all of our daily activities, which exists only in collectives of people, i.e. in states, nations, and organizations. Culture is a system itself. The word "system" derives from the ancient Greek word *systema* which comes from two words – *syn*, which means "together", and *histemi*, which means "to set." System is actually an idea which defines how process or ideology is to be set for the best possible performance or outcome. Cultural or ideological systems can be seen as a collection of roles which reflect human values and thus have a direct impact on organizational results. As a system, culture needs to be viewed using a systematic approach and not a mono-dimensional view.

Three Dimensions of Culture

Culture is multidimensional. One dimension is pragmatic and rational, regulating rules, norms, and codes of working in organizations. A second dimension is more irrational and incorporates the behavioral and psychological approach of the group's members to their duties and to the organization itself. A third dimension reflects the transcendent side of culture, which can be viewed as the organizational cathedral, the reference point for the entire organization's activity.

Regarding the strictly rational aspect, Aristotle wisely defined a state, as an interaction for reaching mutual goals. Not short-term tasks, but goals of successful survival, prosperity, mutual support, defense, and satisfaction of its own needs. Applying Aristotle's definition to an organizational viewpoint, we can say that it is similar to the purpose of the state, just on a smaller scale – an organization is the interaction of its members ordered to reach defined goals that benefit the organization.

Organisational Anatomy (Konovalov 2016, 71) defines organizational culture as a catalyzer of performance. I will use this definition in the present discussion as being the most advanced and practically relevant to the aims of all organizations. Looking at the spiritual or transcendent side, we can consider company culture as the soul of the organizational body, which helps the brain (management) motivate the body for action, sense the environment, attract stakeholders' positive emotions and energy, stimulate and encourage development, and drive the organization through tough times.

This third dimension is the dynamic power and spiritual core of the organization. It is built on symbols which shape the company's psychological state and define the boundaries of its influence. We will discuss the role of symbols and values in more detail later as this is a tremendously critical and under-appreciated issue.

Each of these facets of organizational culture empowers and enlightens the other sides of the immaterial core of any company, and by doing so, gives life and vitality to a company. Culture also defines the boundaries of an organization. Within those boundaries, dependent upon the culture's nature, the talents of the employees are revealed and allowed to flourish.

Indispensable Catalyzer

Production or providing of services can be compared with a complicated chemical reaction of long-chain utilization of resources by perfectly synergized functions. A chemical reaction is a change of two components – substance and energy. Substance, in this sense, represents all tangible and intangible resources and capabilities within an organization. Organizational culture is that energy which comes from the joint efforts and enthusiastic fulfillment of duties of all employees, and, as a result, adds spark and life to all processes. If the culture is positive and stimulating, then we can expect the desired reaction which results in a superior product and secures growth.

At the same time, we do not want culture to be a counterproductive energy, i.e. an inhibitor, which slows down substance transformation, making resource utilization costly and restricting the organization's growth. In a more rigorous way, there is a fit between strategy and culture which has a direct impact on company performance.

In a positive cultural environment, we become more productive and positively attuned toward colleagues. We speak with enthusiasm to friends about what we do, how important it is, and how good it is to work for our company. If the organization's members are effectively collaborating, positively and naturally attuned toward achieving company goals, this positive energy will aid in creating excellent products even if the materials used are less than perfect. Using culture to generate this level of enthusiasm and commitment is important for any company, established or start-up. Strong culture allows enhanced exploitation of people's competencies, reaching higher behavioral consistency among employees, and overall preparedness for necessary change.

Immortal Soul

A strong soul defines a healthy psychological state and provides strength. If one is going through challenges at a stage when muscles are prepared to give up, the soul pushes forward and thus achieves success. Also, it is important to understand that a company and its culture cannot be separated just as a human being and a soul cannot function independently of each other.

A group of people, even when working toward the same goal, remains a crowd without this intangible, yet vital, element of culture. Culture serves as a force which forms productive and collaborative teams. Culture is born as soon as founders start actively interacting in the creation of a business plan and establishing a new venture, even before the organization is fully formed. They are imprinting the first characteristics of culture, its nature and shape. Unfortunately, the issue of culture is usually a neglected conversation by entrepreneurs and start-up enthusiasts, often at the cost of a slow and ineffective start-up. Entrepreneurs and investors need to look into the cultural properties of a new project as a matter of priority, for in so doing, they will define future growth prospects which can predict future performance.

Spiritual Core

The spiritual core defined by culture is responsible for a sense of belonging, loyalty, pride, and a number of other crucial factors of productive organizational citizenship. Residing in symbols and a proclaimed understanding of the need for effective interaction towards organizational goals, cultural identity in any organization is as unique as human fingerprints and cannot be replicated anywhere else.

When we talk about a person we admire, a common characteristic we note is that this person is able to pull him or herself together when facing difficulties. A person who exhibits such spiritual strength is able to deliver extraordinary performance and reveal inner creativity in the face of adversity.

The same applies in businesses where spiritual identity permeates all operations and processes, forming a solid dome above a company, allowing it to withstand any problem. However, if a company's spiritual identity is weak, it is like being under a leaky shelter, eventually driving its people away.

http://wbp.bz/csa

AVAILABLE FROM MICHAEL CORDOVA AND WILDBLUE PRESS!

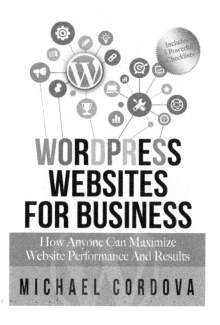

WORDPRESS WEBSITES FOR BUSINESS by MICHAEL CORDOVA

http://wbp.bz/ww4b

Read A Sample Next

The Importance of Long-Tail Keywords, Intent and the Mobile Factor

When you use keyword phrases consisting of several words in them you have a much better chance of getting ranked for those keyword phrases. Not only that, you can incorporate the users intent in them. For example, let's say you were selling golf clubs.

See the following keywords and note how the search terms get more specific and show more intent as you go down:

golf – Someone killing time on their computer

golf clubs – Someone doing general research for golf clubs

pitching wedge – Someone doing general research on pitching wedges

ping G30 driver deals – Someone looking to buy a Ping G30 driver

When doing your keyword research you need to think about what intent you are looking to capture, what specific types of products and services you *want to* provide. Of course it varies by the type of company. Here are some examples of long-tail keywords with intent to engage or purchase:

small business cpa firm to reduce our taxes

auto mechanic to fix my 2017 jeep grand cherokee transmission

chiropractor specializing in a stiff neck

whole roasted pig with green chile catering service (I must be getting hungry)

You need to keep the long-tail and intent concepts in mind when you do your keyword research and write your content. This refinement will make a huge difference in your results. In the above examples, if you instead had focused on cpa firm, auto mechanic, chiropractor or catering service then you'll not only *not be* targeting your company's specific services, but you'll be attempting to rank for keywords that are the most difficult to get top organic rankings for.

Now that we have really smart phones that you can just ask questions of like the Apple Siri or the Android "Ok Google…" capability, and devices like the Amazon Echo (Alexa) and Google Home, search engine queries are now being slanted to those coming from these devices. Now queries like these are becoming more important:

"Ok Google, what's the best Mexican restaurant near me?"

"Alexa, what are the best local activities for kids"

"What are the best local coffee shops"

People are searching on their mobile devices in a hands-free scenario looking for a service that they can use now. *They're on the way!* You need to think about these concepts when you compile your list of keywords that you'll be targeting for your website content.

The Best Tools to Find Long-Tail Keywords

Google again provides great methods and tools to acquire highly relevant long-tail keywords. Since it is Google rankings that you are after, taking Google's suggestions is getting your keywords straight from the horse's mouth.

Do a Google search for your topic and pay attention to the search terms that Google suggests in the search box:

Next, scroll down to the bottom of the results of your search and note the other terms (long-tail keywords) that Google suggests for you:

Searches related to concrete contractor

concrete **contractors denver**	**commercial** concrete **contractors denver**
concrete **delivery denver**	**good day** concrete
residential concrete **denver**	**denver** concrete **prices**
denver concrete **services**	**sunny day** concrete

Grab the keyword phrases that are relevant to your current needs and use them in your article. If you need more then recycle - take the relevant ones and use them in another search to get more suggestions.

A favorite tool among marketers is UberSuggest.io. You just type in a seed keyword, and it gives you a ton of other keywords by appending words to your seed keyword starting with each letter of the alphabet. The video at the bottom of the page shows you how to copy and paste these keywords to a spreadsheet and use all of their basic functions.

Another quick source of long-tail keywords is http://soovle. com. Just type in your keyword and they'll list relevant options from Google, Bing, Yahoo!, Wikipedia, Youtube, Answers.com and Amazon.

Many more keyword tools are available in the free download that you can grab from the Resources section at the end of this book.

Use Qualified, Prioritized Keywords to Drive Compelling Content

Once you have completed the above, then you have the information you need to start mapping out your website content. Create a Wordpress category for each of the categories in the spreadsheet. If a category is too broad, then break it down into multiple categories of finer detail. Sort the spreadsheet by two columns - priority then category. This provides you with the keywords most relevant to your business and the topics (categories) that you can provide solutions for. Next create a list of solutions representing a series of posts for each of the categories. You don't have to write the content now, just a list of concepts/solutions that you'll write about. This list will be your content map for future blog posts. Think in terms of problems that your customers are looking to solve, and solutions that you have already provided *or can provide*.

Ask each member of your team to make a list of the solutions they have provided for customers, then drop each one into the most relevant category. Doing this will provide a great inventory of blog posts that are targeted to solving your customers problems *with your company's priorities built-in*. They'll be customer-centric in terms of solutions to their problems, and they'll be focusing on keywords that are a priority to your business with a great chance of getting rankings and traffic from them.

This is huge, so if you didn't grasp this concept stop now. Go back and read it again. This is all of the content you'll ever need for your website. As you continue to provide solutions, add more content.

http://wbp.bz/ww4b

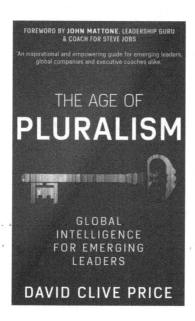
1. TRIBAL TOM-TOMS

Tribalism: a very strong feeling of loyalty to a political or social group, so that you support them whatever they do (Cambridge Dictionary)

I was sitting in the coffee bar of my local gym the day after the wedding of Meghan Markle to Prince Harry and discussing the wedding coverage in the newspapers with Dev, a member of my gym class.

Dev is of Indian descent but he has lived all his life in London, and he works for a big legal firm as a strategic advisor.

'It's all a bit overblown,' said Dev. 'I mean, yes, she has a black mother and a white father, but it's not as if racial discrimination is going to die out overnight just because they've got hitched.'

'No', I said, 'that's very true. But the media have painted it as a symbol of changing times—and I have to say they have a point.'

Dev looked at me quizzically, as if I didn't quite understand the issues at stake. Then he smiled. 'Something tells me you are a true Brit—queen and country and all that. A bit of a royalist?'

I laughed. It was true I did have a sneaking admiration for things royal, history, and traditions, ever since I was a boy. I rather liked pomp and ceremony, at least the way Brits did them (and the French too), and I had studied kings and queens and courts for my history degree.

So yes, I had enjoyed the Royal Wedding—but just as much for what it represented as for what actually took place. It didn't move me because it was royal and British and confirmed my tribal identity.

It moved me because it was interracial and celebratory of mixed heritage. There was a black gospel choir from London singing the spiritual 'This Little Light of Mine'. There was a rousing, evangelist-style sermon from a senior American black bishop, quoting Martin Luther King Jr. There was young, award-winning black cellist Sheku Kanneh-Mason playing Fauré.

And most of all, there was an American actress bride of mixed heritage supported by her cool and elegant mother Doria. And all this within St. George's Chapel at Windsor Castle, attended by the cream of the British establishment.

'But it's not just me, Dev. I think a lot of people liked it, not because it celebrated Britishness. But because the mixed race thing was no big deal. It was kind of, well, normal.'

'Mmmm,' said Dev. 'Let's see how that pans out. One mixed race royal marriage is not going to solve racial discrimination all in one go. People are still going to stick to their tribes.'

'That's true,' I said. 'But most people were more interested in her dress and outfits than her skin colour—isn't that's a sign of progress? I mean, maybe we're starting to grow up. Maybe we're ready to stop defining people simply by what they look like.'

'Or by the tribes they belong to,' said Dev and took a long meaningful sip of his coffee.

In the following days I thought a lot about Dev and that comment about tribes. And I did some research.

It turned out that he was right. According to Trevor Phillips, former chairman of the UK Equality and Human Rights Commission, Britain is now the western country in which interracial marriages are most common. There are more than 1 million dual-heritage Brits, the largest single group being the children of white Brits and people of African or Caribbean descent. By 2030, if the term 'black British' is ever used, it is more likely to mean mixed race. The usual tribal epithets will become irrelevant.

So maybe I was right too. The wedding of Prince Harry and Meghan Markle showed that mixed-race marriages aren't exceptional. Indeed, the problem with dividing the world into tribes is that it leaves out these essential drivers of modern life. In a unique way, the children of mixed marriages combine two different worlds, increasingly at ease in all parts of society rather than being identified by their skin colour or tribe.

We are not defined by simple labels or movements or assumed loyalties. We are not one thing or another. Whatever the politicians and social media and pundits might say, we are not black and white, not even physically. And we cannot hope to influence, guide, and collaborate with other people-especially in our incredibly interconnected world-if we rely on tribal allegiances and readymade categories.

Today's global economy is far too fast moving and fluid to be divided into tribes. However much populist movements and protectionists, nationalists, and nativists try to divide the world based on identity-into tribes of 'them' and 'us', countries and groups, races and religions, local and global-they cannot hold back the tide of pluralism that is sweeping the globe.

And in order to ride this wave, leaders must be able to embrace complexity and change, reach out to other viewpoints and perspectives, and learn to create new combinations and richer amalgams of thought and action.

Most commentators misunderstand the nature of tribes. Their view of them as primitive and insular, even violent, is common in the vocabulary of modern politics. It's as if the recourse to tribalism is some ancient mechanism, a return to an ancestral way of doing things. In our vague anthropology, we think of tribes as imposing unity on individuals by repetitive social customs. Contemporary tribes such as political parties are seen as a natural refuge from inevitable conflict. They are exclusionary and conformist, offering safety in numbers and an admiration of authoritarianism. They believe in their moral superiority.

But as many anthropological studies show, actual tribes are characterized by surprisingly open boundaries. They experiment with other tribes' practices and social forms. They frequently adopt outsiders. Captured white settlers were often invited into the communal life of North American tribes (even staying in the group when liberated).

Among certain tribes in North Africa, members can voluntarily leave their own tribe and join another.

Traditional tribesmen continually create forms of mutual obligation, not only within the tribe but also across tribes. Leaders of the Berbers of North Africa, for example, are commonly chosen or ratified by the group's opponents in the belief that one's current enemy may later be an ally.

Imagine the Republicans and Democrats in the USA choosing the other party's leaders! What would happen if members of the populist right wing and left wing parties of Europe changed loyalties every so often? Many tribes, such as the Mae Enga of Papua New Guinea and the Lozi of Central Africa, even share the practice of marrying members of enemy tribes to reduce the possibility of inter-tribal warfare. Grandchildren are raised in different kinship groups, and a majority of tribes are multilingual due to intermarriage and strong trading relations.

Tribes do not need to be exclusionary to flourish. You might draw parallels with contemporary educational exchange between countries like China and the USA, or the incubator startups and digital entrepreneurs of Bangalore or Silicon Valley or Shanghai. These open groups are much more like traditional tribes in the sense of being built on the cross-fertilization of ideas. They are inherently non-authoritarian, inclusive, and loosely democratic.

The partisan tribes of our contemporary politics are mainly characterized by aggression and, above all, a sense of moral superiority. This is in direct contrast to historical tribes. Most of these groups, as the anthropologist Paul Dresch says of Yemeni tribes, practice an 'avoidance of any absolute judgment, a kind of moral particularism or pluralism.' This is because traditional tribes know that social isolation or claims of moral superiority limit their flexibility. They must be able to adapt to survive. They cannot adapt if they are exclusive, or if they have a rigid set of rules for every situation.

Present day identity politics borrows the warring images of tribes to make our politics much more adversarial than necessary. It seals tribal members off from other tribes and, more damagingly, from the diversity and accelerating technological change that is the reality for thousands of intermingling cultures across the globe. Rather than cutting people off from each other and seeking security in smaller groups-as our current political tribes attempt-we should be embracing the opportunities of collaboration, innovation, and creativity that the global economy presents.

Whether we like it or not, we are now more interconnected than ever before, and we have far less scope for thinking of people far away as 'not like us' or worse, 'stupid'. All the peoples of the world are teaching each other new perspectives, different visions, unexpected connections on a daily basis. You may think of yourself a being part of the post-globalisation wave. You may consider yourself a member of a tribe that has been left behind by the rising tide of globalisation. You may even be anti-globalist.

It doesn't matter. Whether your tribe is for or against globalisation, we are all global citizens now. Rather than seeing the world in terms of tribal or nationalist loyalties, it is much more productive-and tribal in the traditional sense-to think of yourself as a global citizen.

This does not mean that you are a 'citizen of nowhere', as British prime minster Theresa May once declared in relation to international business élites. It does mean that you are plugged into the cultures, perspectives, and customs of people of many backgrounds all across the world. You may be following them on the Internet or via streaming devices. You may be doing business with them. They may be part of your international or virtual team. They may be just round the corner or at the farthest end of the globe. You may access them via translation apps, or simply in the lingua franca of English, Spanish, or Chinese via Skype or Zoom.

However you relate to them, they are part of your daily world and business life. Thinking in purely 'tribal' terms means that you are almost certainly missing out on vast areas of experience and abundance that this extraordinary wired planet of ours now offers. Get over the old tribalism-which is, in fact, a caricature of tribalism. Become a leader in the borderless world that is now at your fingertips!

The leaders of the future must look beyond tribes and borders. They must cultivate an inner curiosity and malleability to thrive in many different cultural situations, and with people of many different backgrounds. When Berber tribes find themselves in a dispute, one group may call on the leader of the other to settle the claim, in the knowledge that he will not risk his ability to form later alliances by supporting his own side.

Now that's what I call global leadership.

2. THE RISE OF THE AMPHIBIANS

Looking back, I guess I always thought of myself as a bit of an amphibian. In every place and culture I went, I sank or swam—and usually swam.

According to the dictionary, the literal definition of amphibian is 'a cold-blooded vertebrate animal of a class that comprises the frogs, toads, newts, salamanders, and caecilians. They are distinguished by having an aquatic gill-breathing larval stage followed typically by a terrestrial lung-breathing adult stage.'

I am not cold blooded (I hope), nor have I moved from breathing through gills to breathing through lungs. But the broader sense of the word, derived from the Greek word amphibious, suggests having two lives or living in both water and on land. This is borne out by the modern adaptation of the noun 'amphibian', meaning a vehicle that is able to move on both land and water, or an aeroplane that can land on both land and water.

So my metaphor of sinking or swimming is reasonably accurate. My parents were born in Wales but I was born in London, so nothing very exotic there. Perhaps I first learned to sink or swim as a 17-year-old grammar school boy going up to Cambridge University, where I found myself surrounded by more mature public school boys. They already had cosmopolitan airs and had the money to travel in their summer vacations.

It was only when I was well into my postgraduate studies that I met my first partner, who happened to be Swiss German. So on finishing my doctorate, I made a big decision. I went to live with Davide and his family in Switzerland—which is when my amphibian instincts took over. I learned Swiss German to converse with my family while I also improved my French. Under the influence of the Swiss Sprachwunder (language miracles) all around me, I also learned rudimentary Italian and helped Davide organize a film festival every year in Locarno, in the Italian part of Switzerland.

From Locarno it seemed just a short step into Italy itself. I was lucky. I managed to obtain a British Academy Travel Fellowship at the University of Bologna, and then went on to lecture on Renaissance history at the European Institute in Florence. Nothing seemed to stop me exploring at that age. Nothing seems to stop young people now, who are, if anything, more amphibious than me. I lived for a while in a converted garage near Bologna station (convenient for trains to the archives in Modena and Mantua). And then together with Davide, I bought a broken-down farmhouse in Tuscany and for a while, I commuted to Florence, while I worked the land for wine and olives, Davide commuted to Locarno, and I began to write my first novel.

It all seemed to happen naturally somehow. One moment I was studying in the cloistered halls of Cambridge University and the next I was a farmer and writer in Italy. And it didn't end there. In order to research that first novel, I eventually decided to take a year off from Tuscany and travel to New York. There I rented a cheap apartment just south of the downtown area of Manhattan called Alphabet City (Avenues A to C). At that time in the early 1980s, the streets to the south of East Houston Street were not entirely safe, but they hosted a richly diverse and not-yet-gentrified sub-culture in which citizens of every race and nation on Earth were gathered in close proximity. Rich terrain to set a novel.

Indeed, New York gave me confidence to celebrate being amphibious, while also giving me the freedom to be creative alongside people from many different backgrounds- Jews, blacks, Hispanics, Eastern Europeans, Chinese, Koreans- who I met there and who seemed to be as amphibious as I was. Perhaps it was no surprise that I met and fell in love with an African American painter while I lived in Alphabet City. My passion was not reciprocated and by the time I returned to Italy, my decade-long relationship with Davide was seriously damaged. It took us another two years to split. I stayed on at the farm to write my book and then Davide encouraged me to seek new pastures in a region of the world that was already fascinating me.

Instead of returning to England, I headed for Tokyo. And then, after a year of finding that I was more sinking than swimming, I followed Davide's generous advice and moved to Hong Kong.

Arriving in this British colony with nothing much more than a PhD and a couple of published books in my luggage, I found work as a economics researcher for the Economist Intelligence Unit. After a couple of years finding my feet, I successfully applied for the position of speechwriter for HSBC, one of the world's leading banks. My remit was to create the key messages for the handover of Hong to China in July 1997. I also met Simon, a young Hong Kong Chinese man who was in a group of friends who came to the airport to greet me on my arrival from Tokyo. I have been together with him ever since.

So yes, I became an Asian amphibian. In order to explore my new family and their culture, I lived together with Simon's mother, sister, and nephew in their small apartment in a Kowloon housing estate. In that way I really got to know about Chinese daily life, festivals, and customs, even as I took a taxi each morning to work in the shiny HSBC headquarters in the Central financial district.

One of the big benefits of being in a multinational was that I could continue my work as a freelance writer in my spare time and long vacations. So I travelled extensively in South Korea, Japan, Myanmar, China, Thailand, all the while writing books and articles. Throughout this period I also continued to adopt the same amphibious approach as I had in Europe: Swim, David! Don't sink!

Indeed, I have continued to live like this ever since: being ready to explore in a new culture, having one foot here and one foot there, getting adopted by locals or even a whole family. In so doing, I have often found myself an outsider, on the edge of a culture where I can communicate both ways—into and out of the group. But whereas I once thought I was one of a lucky few who sought out these hybrid experiences, now I think it is quite commonplace.

This is especially true of the young leaders and potential leaders of today. It's amazing how many millennials now seem to be of mixed background. I've lost count of the number of people who tell me they are Third Culture Kids or TCKs. This term, first used by sociologist Ruth Hill Useem in the 1950s for children raised in a culture other than their parents' (or the culture of a country given on a child's passport), has become a mark of pride for many people of mixed parentage.

I was recently coaching an executive who was brought up in his father's native country of Brazil. He speaks Portuguese and English, but currently lives in California near his mother, managing two trading teams in Singapore and Malaysia. He calls himself a TCK and was rather aggrieved that he wasn't getting the results he deserved from his Southeast Asia teams, 'even though I am used to adapting to other cultures.'

I have another colleague, Eric, who is married to a Japanese woman, but who spent several years in Shanghai and has a Chinese mother and a French father. He speaks Mandarin, French, and English, and now lives and works in London and New York. His children speak English, French, and Mandarin. Perhaps unsurprisingly, he is an expert in international start-ups.

This amphibiousness seems to have become more marked as the pace of technological change, international travel, interracial marriage, matrix working, and social media quickens. Not only is everyone connected, but also several life experiences are connected within one person or one family.

Amphibians are pluralism personified. However, pluralism isn't just living with difference, or tolerating difference, or even celebrating difference. It's discovering that you have roots here but also there, a dynamic that creates a third personality. 'Being hyphenated can sometimes cause problems,' one TCK told me. 'But it's also fun.'

I am not officially hyphenated but my hybrid experiences have made a coherent identity of all my influences. Of course it might not be so much fun for others, such as expatriate executives, who are sometimes relocated time and again because they haven't been able to work in the prevailing culture.

I can think of many people in the multinationals where I've worked, or executive clients who have been discomfited by new cultural situations, new members of their international teams, or new in-country assignments where they simply have not 'gelled'. Failing in Japan or Saudi Arabia or Mexico (or on the East and West Coasts of the US) costs companies huge amounts of money in replacement costs and also in repatriating disgruntled executives, who may well leave the company in the aftermath of disappointment.

Research shows that some 65 per cent of expatriates fail in the first or second posting, while 90 per cent of global executives identify cross-cultural effectiveness as their biggest challenge.

Clearly, there are many professionals out there who are non-amphibians. However, the more you look around the more you see examples of interesting and hybrid backgrounds, especially among the often well-travelled and footloose younger generation. These are our future leaders. And although they may not be ready for leadership yet, many of them are already tending towards that edge-of-the-group mindset and appreciation of mixed influences where creativity flourishes. If you look at Western media, TV, and films-or even Japanese, Korean, or Latin American media and films-you will see mixed race, mixed sexuality, and mixed backgrounds portrayed on the screen now far more than ever before.

Our Master Chef and Celebrity Bake-off programmes on UK television are full of exotic 'fusion' dishes from cuisines all over the world. The contestants are British-born Somalis and Nigerians, Indians, Chinese, Sri Lankans, Columbians, Cypriots, Italians, and many others of diverse backgrounds. It's perhaps no surprise that it is these contestants who are often the most creative.

But what really makes an amphibian succeed? What makes one person flourish in diverse situations and cultures, some of them far removed from anything they have experienced before, while another is like a fish out of water? What are the main drivers that are making the amphibians thrive with every fresh experience of difference?

http://wbp.bz/aopa

CPSIA information can be obtained
at www.ICGtesting.com
Printed in the USA
LVHW081542140820
663197LV00023B/2985